THE COVENANT WOMAN
OF THE NEW TESTAMENT

A Book about Bible Women for Modern Women

By Nancy Evelyn Allen

PUBLISHED BY WESTVIEW, INC. NASHVILLE, TENNESSEE

© 2009 Nancy Allen
All Rights Reserved, including the right to reproduction,
in whole or in part, in any form.
ISBN 978-1-935271-21-5
August 2009

Every effort has been made to trace copyrights on materials included in this publication. If any copyrighted material has been included without permission and due acknowledgment, proper credit will be inserted in future printings after notice has been received.

Printed in the United States of America on acid free paper.

PUBLISHED BY WESTVIEW, INC.
P.O. Box 210183,
Nashville, Tennessee 37221
www.publishedbywestview.com

CONTENTS

Volume Two:
The Covenant Woman of the New Testament

ACKNOWLEDGMENTS v
PREFACE vii

Part One: Walking with Jesus
CONCORDANCE FOR PART ONE 3
CHAPTER I. Women in the Synoptic Gospels 15
CHAPTER II. Women in Jesus' Childhood 19
CHAPTER III. Jesus' Ministry of Healing and
    Compassion—-Demons 33
CHAPTER IV. Jesus' Ministry of Healing and
    Compassion—Disease 41
CHAPTER V. Jesus' Ministry of Healing and
    Compassion—Death 49
CHAPTER VI. Women Who Ministered With Jesus 55
CHAPTER VII. Lessons Taught Through Women 77

Part Two: Growing the Church
CONCORDANCE FOR PART TWO 93
CHAPTER I. The Church 120
CHAPTER II. Lessons for Women from
    Early Church Writers 143

CHAPTER III. Women in Leadership Roles 147
CHAPTER IV. Women in Support Roles 167
CHAPTER V. Women's Actions that Teach 175
CHAPTER VI. Consummated 187

BIBLIOGRAPHY 195

ACKNOWLEDGMENTS

My humble appreciation and thanks goes out to so many people who encouraged and helped me with this book: First to my husband who suffered through every version and rewrite. A thank you to all the people who read and offered their advise and comments; Chris Allen, Bea Robins, Mert Veech, Ray Waddell, Shirley Green and Beverly Duncan. Thanks to Joyce Myers, Bill Craig and Harold Brown for offering their encouragement. Debbie Karnes helped with the computer and formatting. My editor, Mary Catharine Nelson, has done an extraordinary job on a very difficult manuscript.

Finally, thank you to the Nolensville United Methodist women's group who first asked me to teach a class on the women of the Bible. God used them to get me started writing and has sustained the desire within me to bring this work to completion. Thanks be to God.

PREFACE

The intent of this book is not to disparage men, but rather to bring women face to face with men in parallel equality. God, Himself, initiated the reciprocal oneness of human relationship when He brought Eve to Adam and placed her in front of him. Woman came from man and henceforth mankind comes from woman.

This concept, however, is more profound than human marriage. God created Adam and Eve in His own Image. God's Image is not only male, but also female! This Image of God embraces both genders!

From the onset of the Scriptures to the consummation, God is leading His readers to encounter His image, embrace Him in relationship and declare their love for Him in a marriage that is undefiled. Therefore, God has used both males and females when calling and shaping a people to be His own. The first women laid the foundations. It was through the women that nations were formed and it was through the right women that the promise was given. Although cultural norms often put limits on women, both the Old and New Covenants highlight *covenant women* who were used to further God's purpose. It is profoundly evident that the women's stories in the Old and New Covenants play a vital role in sustaining the Jewish and Christian faiths.

To facilitate study, with each major thrust, women are grouped together in order to acclimatize the readers and students to the times and circumstances from which the Bible women functioned. The *Bible Book Summary* is intended as a resource to bring harmony to the scene and provide a look into how God and the writers used the female in their script. Given the wide range of options about dates, the dates recorded herein are provided for the sole purpose of chronological narrative. At the end of each chapter there is a side bar called *21st Century Perspective* and another called, *To Ponder*, with questions to aid in making the story personal to the readers. Finally, a study guide is provided *For the Teacher*, featuring four steps: *Introduction, Instruction, Internalize and Infold.*

Women through the ages have a common bond. We are wives, mothers, daughters, grandmothers, granddaughters, mothers-in-law and daughters-in-law, aunts, nieces, and cousins. Women live in relationship. We function within our cultures. We work and play, give and take, cry and laugh, and while we are fulfilling our obligations to our fellowman and society, our highest calling remains the same: We are to love God with our whole being. The *bride of Christ* knows no gender. God does not allow for excuses. We belong to Him and we are invited to the marriage supper. (Revelation 19:9)

It is my desire that women everywhere will accept God's marriage proposal!

Volume Two, Part One

WALKING WITH JESUS

PART ONE
CONCORDANCE

THE BOOK OF MATTHEW

(The man who wrote it and the women who helped shape it)

Matthew: The Man

Levi likely had seen Jesus, heard His message and perhaps knew Him personally before the day Jesus called him from his *tax office* to be His Disciple. (Matthew 9:9; Mark 2:14; Luke 5:27) Levi's willingness to follow Jesus in reckless abandonment appears to be without regard for his work or family. We are told he was a tax collector and he worked for the Roman government, holding a position that was not respected because tax collectors in general made their money by defrauding the people: "The Pharisees and their scribes murmured against his [Jesus'] disciples, saying, *why do you eat and drink with tax collectors and sinners?*" (Luke 5:30) Matthew had invited his fellow tax collectors over to his house for dinner and also invited Jesus to be his honored guest. Matthew immediately shared his new-found faith with his friends. While the Pharisees saw them as unacceptable company, Jesus saw no harm in sharing a meal with them. He associated with the unacceptable in order to make them acceptable. Perhaps Levi changed his name to Matthew (gift of Yahweh) after he became a follower of Jesus.

Matthew brought many skills to the ministry of Jesus. He was accustomed to the business world, knew how to organize, write and keep records. He must have been a blessing to his fellow Apostles, and it must have been a blessing for him to have talents that could be used in service to his Lord.

Matthew: The Book

While Matthew, the man, never appears first in the list of Apostles, "in the early church Matthew, the book, was the most highly valued and widely read of the four Gospels." (*Pictorial Bible Dictionary*, p. 516.) "The titles to the Gospels were not added until the 2nd century." (*Holman Bible Handbook*, p. 541.) The early church attributed the book to Matthew; however, it is possible that it was written by someone who used a source written by Matthew. The dates of authorship range from 40 to 115 A.D. However, the book of Matthew was likely written after Mark and possibly before the fall of Jerusalem in 70 A. D. The book derives its substance from at least three sources: The Book of Mark which forms the framework, a Q source of 250 verses and sayings of Jesus, and the M source unique to Matthew. The text was written in Greek but shows signs of having been translated from Aramaic. Therefore, the author wrote for Greek-speaking individuals who likely had Hebrew backgrounds. "He used Old Covenant *proof text* 130 times to establish Jesus as the expected Messiah, King of the Jews and the son of David." (*Jesus, The Man, The Mission, And The Message*, p. 78) To Matthew, "the Gospel was the *New Law* and Jesus was the *second Moses*." (Ibid., p. 78.) The primary concerns of the Book of Matthew are pastoral and didactic rather than theological. The early church found the book helpful for instruction and care. Perhaps this is the reason Matthew has taken first place at the head of the New Covenant.

FEMALES IN THE BOOK OF MATTHEW:

Matthew places women in somewhat less favor than does Luke. Perhaps he takes a more traditional Jewish viewpoint. Mary is almost always *the wife of* or *the mother of*. It is the man's household (10:36); however, Matthew does report the healing of the Canaanite woman's daughter. Women and children also ate at the feeding of the 4000, (15:38) and he shows parallel equality in marriage and parenting, (19:4-5,19); two men in a field and two women grinding (24:40-41); the five wise virgins and the two wise men who invested their talents (25:2, 16,17); the slave in the garden and the maid in the courtyard (26:51, 69); Pilate and his wife (27:19-24); Joseph from Arimathea, Mary Magdalena and the other women at the tomb of Jesus. (27:59-61)

Tamar 1:3
Rahab 1:5
Ruth 1:5
Wife of Uriah 1;6
Husband of Mary 1:16
His mother 1:18; 2:11, 13, 19; 12:46
Mary 1:18, 20; 2:11; 13:55
Your wife 1:20
Virgin 1:23
Rachel 2:18
Woman 5:28; 9:20; 13:33; 15:28; 22:26; 26:7
His wife 5:31; 18:25; 19:5, 9-10; 22:25; 27:19

Divorced woman 5:32
Mother-in-law 8:14; 10:35
My daughter 9:18; 15:22
Daughter 9:22; 10:35, 37
Girl 9:24-25; 14:11
Daughter-in-law 10:35
Mother 10:37; 12:50; 13:55; 19:19, 29
Women 11:11; 14:21; 15:38; 28:5
Queen of the South 12:42
My mother 12:48-49
Sister 12:50
Sisters 13:56; 19:29
Philip's wife 14:3
The daughter of Herodias 14:6

Herodias 14:6
Her mother 14:8, 11
Your mother 15:4-5
Canaanite woman 15:22
Her daughter 15:28
One's wife 19:3
Female 19:4
Wives 19:8
Mother of the sons of
    Zebedee 20:20; 27:56
Daughter of Zion 21; 5
Harlots 21:31

Widow 22:24
Two women 24:41
Ten maidens 25:1
Maidens 25:7, 11
Maid 26:69, 71
Many women 27:55
Mary Magdalene 27:56,
    61; 28:1
Mary the mother of James
    and Joseph 27:56
Other Mary 27:61; 28:1

THE BOOK OF MARK

(The man who wrote it and the women who helped shape it)

Mark: The Man

Perhaps as a boy, John Mark witnessed Jesus on the eve of His trial being taken away to the high priest. He reports what appears to be a first-hand experience: "A young man followed him [Jesus] with nothing but a linen cloth about his body; and they seized him, but he left the linen cloth and ran away naked." (Mark 14:51) Mark likely would have been familiar with Jesus and his Disciples because his mother provided her home for prayer meetings and hospitality. After Jesus was crucified, one such prayer meeting took place for Peter who was imprisoned. When an angel set Peter free, the first place Peter went was to Mary's house. (Acts 12:12)

It seems only natural that Mark's cousin, Barnabas, would take him under his wing and so Mark accompanied Barnabas and Paul on their first missionary journey. (Acts 13:13) However, the arrangement did not work out. John Mark left the group in Perga of Pamphylia and returned home to Jerusalem. This did not set well with Paul, and hence Paul refused to take Mark on his second journey. Therefore, Barnabas took Mark with him to his native Cyprus while Paul and Silas went to Asia Minor. The split between Paul and Barnabas may not have been entirely Mark's fault; however, because Peter, Barnabas and Paul had a disagreement earlier in Antioch. (Galatians 2:13) Later Mark was found back in Paul's good graces as he was working with Paul while Paul was under house arrest in Rome. (Philemon 24) Again Paul commends Mark as *one who has been a comfort to him,* (Colossians 4:11) and he advised Timothy to "get Mark and bring him with you; for he is very useful in serving me." (II Timothy 4:11)

It is obvious that Mark looked up to Peter, and apparently the feeling was mutual. Peter called Mark *my son.* (I Peter 5:13) Peter and Mark served together in Rome. Although the Bible does not mention a church in Egypt, tradition has it John Mark carried the Gospel message to Egypt and founded the church in Alexandria. (*Pictorial Bible Dictionary*, p. 510.) The *winged lion* is an "emblem dedicated to John Mark [and] can be seen in Mark's paternal city of Venice where he is buried, and there is also a sequence of mosaics of him dating from the thirteenth century in Capella Zeno." (*Oxford Dictionary of the Bible*, p. 242.)

Mark: The Book

"Mark is the first written Gospel, the most basic and the shortest of the four Gospels. It remained the only Gospel for perhaps two decades." (*Jesus, The Man, The Mission, and The Message*, p.75.) Scholars range in opinion, between 40 and 70 A.D., as to the date of writing. The consensus is broadly held that the work was written in Rome. Matthew used 90% of Mark's material and Luke used 50% of Mark's material. However, Mark relied on his own first-hand knowledge, Peter's reliable eye witness testimony and a collection of teachings and sayings that could have been the *Q* source. Several of the early church fathers spoke of Mark writing down what Peter preached.

One can only imagine how Mark reported events close to his heart, such as conflict and reconciliation like he had experienced with Paul. Much of Mark's work appears to be unpolished. Indeed, Matthew and Luke improved his grammar, refined his style and removed what they considered to be unacceptable language. However, Mark was younger and less experienced, so he wrote what he saw and felt. That fact in itself makes the Book of Mark more valuable to his readers, although in the early church Mark received less attention than Matthew and Luke, today, it is the "logical place to begin a study of the Gospels because it holds the basic message of the primitive church." (*Pictorial Bible Dictionary*, p. 511.)

FEMALES IN THE BOOK OF MARK:

Jesus healed Simon's mother-in-law. (1:23, 30) A teenage girl was raised from the dead and a woman was healed from hemorrhaging. (5:2f, 25f, 41-42) Women were not mentioned in the feeding of the 4000 or the 5000. (8:9; 6:44) Fathers and mothers are to be honored and cared for, (7:10-13; 10:19) and Jesus healed the daughter of a Greek woman. (7:25f) God made male and female, (10:6) said to leave father and mother (10:7) and divorces his wife, or if she divorces her husband. (10:11-12) Both rich people and poor widows are mentioned, (12:41-42) and there is female imagery about the last days: birth-pangs (13:8); those with child, those who give suck (13:17); and the woman who anointed Jesus for burial. (14:8) There was a man-servant in the garden and a maid-servant in the courtyard. (14:47, 66) Joseph of Arimathea and the women from Galilee were at the cross and tomb. (15:40-43) Jesus appeared first to Mary Magdalene (16:9) then to two others (16:12) Mark consistently gives witness to the fact that women participated alongside men both in receiving and providing ministry.

Mother-in-law 1:30
His mother 3:31
My mother 3:33-34
Sister 3:35
Mother 3:35; 5:40; 10:7, 19, 29
Little daughter 5:23; 7:25
Woman 5:25, 33; 7:25, 26; 12:22; 14:3
Daughter; 5:34
Your daughter; 5:35; 7:29
Talithe Cumi 5:41
Little girl 5:41
Girl; 5:42 6:22, 28
Son of Mary 6:3
Sisters 6:3; 10:29, 30
Herodias; 6:17, 19
Philip's wife; 6:17
Brother's wife 6:18
Herodias' daughter 6:22
Her mother 6:24, 28
Your mother 7:10-12
Her daughter 7:26

His wife 10:2, 7, 11
Female; 10:6
She divorces her husband 10:12
Mothers 10:29
Wife 12:19, 23
Widows' houses 13:40
Poor widow 12:42-43
Those who are with child 13:17
Those who give suck 13:17
Maids 14:66-69
Women 15:40
Mary Magdalene 15:40, 47; 16:1, 9
Mary the mother of James the younger, Joses, and Salome 15:40, 47; 16:1
Salome 15:40; 16:1
Many other women 15:41

THE BOOK OF LUKE

(The man who wrote it and the women who helped shape it)

Luke: The Man

Luke was a Gentile, perhaps from Macedonia. He most likely attended medical school in Philippi. He was a physician and a first-rate historian with a desire for ministry. He was often found in the company of Paul. "And a vision appeared to Paul in the night: a man of Macedonia was standing beseeching him and saying, *come over to Macedonia and help us.* And when he had seen the vision, immediately *we* sought to go on into Macedonia, concluding that God had called *us* to preach the gospel to them." (Acts 16:9-10)

Luke included himself in this preaching mission to Macedonia. He was traveling with the missionary group in Troas, (Acts 20:5) Cos, Rhodes, Patara, Tyre, Ptolemais, Caesarea and on to Jerusalem where he stayed with a person named Mnason. (Acts 21:16)

There is no evidence Luke did or did not continue to practice medicine while spreading the Gospel. His family is also not mentioned. Tradition informs us he suffered martyrdom in Greece. (*Pictorial Bible Dictionary*, p. 495.)

Luke: The Book

The Book of Luke is the first of a two-part work which includes The Acts of the Apostles. In the style of a historian, Luke first wrote the account of Jesus' life and ministry beginning with John the Baptist and ending with the final events in Jerusalem. (Luke 19:45-24:53) His follow-up manuscript covered the events surrounding the birth and growth of the church.

Luke is a personal gospel highlighting concerns for the disadvantaged and despised. His "message of hope for the oppressed certainly does apply to women, who in every age have been the poor in the population." (*Oxford Dictionary of the Bible*, p. 235.) Also, in the Acts of the Apostles, Luke exalts womanhood, an emphasis natural enough if in fact he was from Macedonia where women were held in high regard. He tells of how Jesus had compassion on women, recalling how Jesus called women to be His Disciples, to *learn at His feet* and to participate in His ministry. It appears as if Luke knew Mary, the mother of Jesus, personally, and perhaps she told Luke the story of Jesus' birth. Luke claims "to compile a narrative of the things which have been accomplished among us, just as they were delivered to us by those who from the beginning were eyewitnesses and ministers of the word." (Luke 1:12)

While the Book of Luke is the last of the Synoptic Gospels to be written, it is believed to have been written between 60 and 80 A.D. for Gentile Christians. "No one knows the locale from which Luke wrote his Gospel." (*Holman Bible Handbook*, p. 585.)

Luke wrote so that Theophilus and others like him might understand that Jesus and Christianity are a natural extension of Judaism, that Jesus is for people of all social classes, genders, races and nations. The church is the *New Israel*, and Jesus endorsed a *New Covenant* to which God is bound and faithful.

FEMALES IN THE BOOK OF LUKE:

More so than any of the other Gospel writers, Luke wrote about and for women. He addressed women's issues and included women in parallel equality beside men: Mary was enrolled with Joseph in Bethlehem (2:4); [Jesus' earthly father and mother] marveled about what was said about him (2:33); the genealogy in Luke is thought to be maternal (3:23-38); the Gentile woman of Zarepath and Naaman the leper were both helped by God (4:26-27); a man with an unclean spirit and Simon's mother-in-law were both healed (4:33, 38). Jesus healed the centurion's slave (7:2) and raised the widow's son (7:15). Both John the Baptist and the *woman sinner* who anointed Jesus understood Jesus' mission. Women and men were cured of demons. (8:2, 27) A woman and a man cried out from the crowd. (9:38 and 11:27) There are also sayings and demonstrations including women alongside men: a mother against her daughter, and a father against his son, etc. (12:53); two women grinding and two men praying (17:35 and 18:10); the rich givers and the poor widow who gave all. (21:1-2) There was a manservant in the Mount of Olives and a maidservant in the courtyard (22:39, 50, 56) and lastly Joseph of Arimathea and the women from Galilee at Jesus tomb. (23:50, 55) Luke follows a story about a man with a story about a woman which shows Jesus was inclusive in His ministry.

Wife 1:5; 14:20; 18:29; 20:28, 33
Daughters of Aaron 1:5
Elizabeth 1:5, 7, 13, 24, 36, 40-41, 57
Your wife 1:13
His mother's womb 1:15
My wife 1:18
His wife 1:24; 16:18
Virgin 1:27
Virgin's name 1:27
Mary 1:27, 30, 34, 38, 39, 41, 45, 56; 2:5, 16, 34
Your kinswoman 1:36

THE COVENANT WOMAN

Handmaid 1:38
Women 1:42; 7:28; 8:2; 23:27, 49, 55; 24:24
Mother of my Lord 1:43
Handmaiden 1:48
Her neighbors and kinsfolk 1:58
His mother 1:60; 2:33-34, 48, 51; 7:12, 15; 8:19
Prophetess 2:36
Anna 2:36
Daughter of Phanuel 2:36
Widow 2:37; 4:26; 7:12; 18:3, 5
Herodias 3:19
Brother's wife 3:19
Woman 4:26; 7:37, 59; 8:43, 47; 10:38; 11:27; 13:11—12, 16, 21; 15:8; 16:18; 20:32-33; 22:57
Simon's mother-in-law 4:38
Mary, called Magdalene 8:2; 14:10
Joanna 8:3; 24:10
Wife of Chuza 8:3
Susanna 8:3
Your mother 8:20
My mother 8:21
Only daughter 8:42
Daughter; 8:48 12:53
Your daughter; 8:49
Mother of the child 5:51
Martha 10:38, 40-41
Sister 10:39
Mary 10:39; 10:42
My sister 10:40
The queen of the South 11:31
Mother 12:53; 14:26
Mother-in-law 12:53
Daughter-in-law 12:53
Daughter of Abraham 13:16
Hen 13:34
Sisters 14:26
Harlots 15:30
Lot's wife 17:32
Two women 17:35
Widows' houses 20:47
Poor widow 21:2—3
Those with child 21:23
Those who give suck 21:23
Maid 22:56
Daughters of Jerusalem 23:28
Mary the mother of James 24:10
Other women 24:10
Some women 24:22

Part One, Chapter One, Lesson Twenty

WOMEN IN THE SYNOPTIC GOSPELS

THE SYNOPTIC GOSPELS

The Gospel or *Good News* about Jesus Christ is told in the first four books of the New Covenant: Matthew, Mark, Luke and John. The first three are called the Synoptic Gospels because they are alike in tone and source. Each Gospel is unique in purpose. For example, Matthew wrote mostly for the Jews and presents *proof text* to convince the Jews that Jesus is the Messiah. The Book of Mark was the first to be written and therefore is the basis for some of the information in the other Gospels. Luke is especially kind to women and Gentiles.

The entire Gospel of Jesus: Jesus was born; Jesus grew physically and spiritually; Jesus taught and made disciples; Jesus was crucified, died and was buried; God raised Jesus from the dead; Jesus ascended into Heaven; and Jesus will return to claim his bride—can be told through the stories and lives of the women who walked with Him.

How wonderful it must have been to have held the baby named Jesus. What a privilege to have been Anna, waiting in the temple to bless the Messiah. And as Jesus grew and was about His Father's business, Mary had the incredible responsibility to discipline her Son for not informing His earthly parents of his whereabouts.

Jesus was about thirty years old when He began His public ministry. He touched women and they touched Him. He spoke to women: Jews, Gentiles, Samaritans and Canaanites alike. He healed women of both mental and physical illnesses. He raised women from the dead, fed them and ate with them, accepted assistance from them, taught them, visited them in their homes, died on the cross for the sins of women, appeared to them after God raised Him from the dead, and shared the ascension with them.

Jesus did not exclude women from any part of His ministry. God intended for women to be equal partners with men, and Jesus went about renewing the original covenant God made with Ish and Ishshah before the Fall. The women who followed Him were married and single, rich and poor, reformed prostitutes and merchants. Is it any wonder women in the first century and throughout the ages have looked forward with excitement to His return?

Many stories about women in the New Covenant demonstrate what the Kingdom of God is like and how it will grow. These stories show God's love, salvation and forgiveness are for everyone including women sinners and foreign women. Jesus allowed women to be taught and recognized their calling to do the work of spreading the Gospel. Women are called to follow Jesus; they followed Jesus in the first century and they follow Him in the twenty-first century. The *Great Commission* speaks to every follower of Jesus: "Go therefore and make disciples of all nations, baptizing them in the name of the Father and of the Son and of the Holy Spirit, teaching them to observe all that I have commanded you." (Matthew 28:19-20)

> ### 21st Century Perspective
>
> The Synoptic Gospel authors wrote their stories about Jesus from first hand experiences and testimonials of eye witnesses. The books of Matthew, Mark and Luke, written in the 1st century, tell accurate and dependable stories about the Messiah. Today the Gnostic Gospels have gained popularity. However, they were written in the 2nd and 3rd centuries and are heavily influenced by embellishments and therefore, were not chosen for the canon.

TO PONDER:

Read: Matthew 1:1-17; Mark 1:1-14; Luke 1:1-4

- ❖ Why did Matthew write?
- ❖ Why did Mark write?
- ❖ Why did Luke write?
- ❖ Think about how these Gospel writers have impacted your life.
- ❖ Which writer speaks to you? How?

Part One, Chapter Two, Lesson Twenty-One

WOMEN IN JESUS' CHILDHOOD

WOMEN IN JESUS' CHILDHOOD

Precious little is written in the Bible about Jesus' childhood. Perhaps it is enough for us to know He is the pre-existent Son of God. He was involved in the creation of all things, (John 1:1-3) and He became human in order to identify with mankind so He could provide a way of salvation. "Though He was in the form of God, did not count equality with God a thing to be grasped, but emptied himself, taking the form of a servant, being born in the likeness of men." (Philippians 2:6-7) Jesus was placed in the womb of a devout young woman named Mary only a short time after the miraculous conception of John the Baptist to Elizabeth and Zechariah. Mary and Elizabeth were close and Mary visited with Elizabeth during their pregnancies. Mary was very young and Elizabeth was growing old. Perhaps Mary learned from Elizabeth about how to care for herself and her child during her pregnancy.

As a baby, born in a stable, Jesus was wrapped in strips of cloth. At the appropriate time, as the law required, his parents took Him to the Temple for a dedication ceremony. There He was blessed by Anna and Simeon. (Luke 2:27-39) By the time the Wise Men visited Jesus, He must have been walking and talking. One wonders if He was a *terrible two* and how He tolerated the long trip to Egypt when Mary and Joseph fled to protect Jesus from King Herod. (Matthew 2:13) "It is perhaps significant that On is named as the place of sojourn of the holy family after the flight into Egypt." (*Pictorial Bible Dictionary*, p. 609) On, Egypt was important in Israel's past because Joseph's wife, Asenath, came from there and the town was known to be a safe place for outsiders. After the family returned from Egypt, Jesus grew up in Nazareth, learning carpentry from Joseph. By the age of twelve, He was about His *real* Father's business and was found in the Temple conversing with the teachers. (Luke 2:41-49)

We hear nothing of His teenage years or His young adult life. However, those years of observation and contemplation served Him well during His ministry, as evidenced by the lessons and examples He used to teach which came from the countryside where He lived during those years. The Bible only tells us, "Jesus increased in wisdom and in stature, and in favor with God and man." (Luke 2:52)

MARY, THE MOTHER OF JESUS

Matthew 1:18-25; Mark 3:31-35; Luke 1:26-56

At least seven centuries before Jesus Christ was born, Isaiah prophesied that a young maiden (it would have been unheard of for a young maiden in that time not to have been a virgin) would bear a son and call his name Immanuel (God with us). Matthew wrote to the Jews in Matthew 1:22-23 that Jesus was the expected Messiah, and he quoted Isaiah 7:14 as a *proof text*.

Luke 1:26f tells us the angel, Gabriel, was sent by God to Mary who was betrothed to Joseph. "According to ancient tradition, her parents were two holy persons, Joachim and Anna." (*All the Women of the Bible*, p. 162.) Mary had at least one sister. (John 19:25) Women often married young in those days, and it appears Mary was no exception. She could have been as young as fifteen and puzzled by Gabriel, as he told her, "do not be afraid, Mary, for you have found favor with God. And behold, you will conceive in your womb and bear a son, and you shall call his name Jesus. He will be great, and will be called the Son of the Most High; and the Lord God will give to him the throne of his father David, and he will reign over the house of Jacob forever; and of his kingdom there will be no end." (Luke 1:30-33; II Samuel 7:14-16) Mary wanted to know how this could happen since she had never had sex. Gabriel said, "The Holy Spirit will come upon you, and the power of the Most High (Elelyon) will overshadow you; therefore the child to be born will be called holy, the Son of God." (Luke 1:35)

Matthew 1:18-25 tells the story from Joseph's perspective: "Now the birth of Jesus Christ took place in this way. When his mother Mary had been betrothed to Joseph, before they came together she was found to be with child of the Holy Spirit; and her husband Joseph, being a just man and unwilling to put her to shame, resolved to divorce her quietly. But as he considered this, behold an angel of the Lord appeared to him in a dream, saying, *Joseph, son of David, do not fear to take Mary your wife, for that which is conceived in her is of the Holy Spirit; she will bear a son, and you shall call his name Jesus, for he will save his people from their sins.* All this took place to fulfill what the Lord had spoken by the prophet: *Behold, a virgin shall conceive and bear a son, and his name shall be called Emmanuel* (God with us). When Joseph woke from sleep, he did as the angel of the Lord commanded him; he took his wife, but knew her not until she had borne a son; and he called his name Jesus."

Mary went to see Elizabeth who was perhaps her cousin. She recognized Mary as a woman blessed of God. (Luke 1:41-45) Mary then praised the Lord with words from her foremother, Hannah: (I Samuel 2:1-10) Mary, being a faithful Jew, would have known the Old Covenant. The Scripture known as *The Magnificat* is Mary's song:

"My soul magnifies the Lord, and my spirit rejoices in God my Savior, for he has regarded the low estate of his hand-maiden. For behold, henceforth all generations will call me blessed; for he who is mighty has done great things for me, and holy is his name. And his mercy is on those who fear him from generation to generation. He has shown strength with his arm, he has scattered the proud in the imagination of their hearts, he has put down the mighty from their thrones, and exalted those of low degree; he has filled the hungry with good things, and the rich he has sent empty away. He has helped his servant Israel, in remembrance of his mercy, as he spoke of our fathers, to Abraham and to his posterity for ever." (Luke 1:46-55)

Mary stayed with her cousin, Elizabeth, for about three months. Mary was betrothed to Joseph. It was assumed by society of the times all women would marry; however, men were often older when they married. A woman was given a dowry and much was made of her beauty. "Although men were encouraged to marry in order to produce children, it was not necessarily expected." (*Jewish Marriage in Antiquity*, p.21.) However, "female asceticism was a growing phenomenon during the time of Christ." (Ibid., p.20.) And, Paul advocated remaining single when possible. (I Corinthians 7:34, 38) So with the coming of Jesus more options were open for women. But, Mary would have had few choices other than marriage.

Mary's trust in God was amazing. She took on the challenge and trusted God to produce the results. He came through for her! Joseph, too, was amazing. He trusted God and gave Mary the protection she needed. And, they did not have sex until after Jesus was born. In verse 25 the word *until* has caused some disagreement among scholars. In Catholic teaching, the Semitic idiom in the use of *until* does not imply they had conjugal relations after the birth of

Jesus. (Notes, Matthew 1:18-2:23, RSV) Protestants believe Jesus had siblings and the word *until* means they had conjugal relations after Jesus was born. Matthew 13:55-56 list siblings: Simon, James, Joseph, Judas and sisters and other references to siblings are Mark 6:3; and Galatians 1:19.

After traveling more than seventy miles from Nazareth to Bethlehem, Mary gave birth to Jesus in a stable. People traveled along trade routes on foot or by animals. The roadside was lawless and dangerous. (*Pictorial Bible Dictionary*, p. 866.) As far as we know, Jesus' birth was unaccompanied by doctors or midwives, pain killers or medication. Some believe Mary and Joseph were denied comforts because there was no room in the inn. On the other hand, God was gracious and loving in providing them a private place with clean straw and the sounds of nature as opposed to an open court where many people would be spending the night: "An Oriental inn bore little resemblance to a hotel today. It was a mere shelter for man and beast. Like the modern *khan* or *caravanserai* it was a large quadrangular court into which admission was gained by a strong gateway." (*Pictorial Bible Dictionary*, p. 375.)

Jesus' birth was private, but God announced His coming from the heavens! Shepherds and wise men alike came to celebrate His birth! (Luke 2:15-16; Matthew 2:1-2)

Mary was a sober, trusting young woman. However, she couldn't help having questions. How could she take in all that was happening to her and her child? She kept all these things *pondering them in her heart*. (Luke 2:19)

Mary and Joseph followed the Law of Moses and had Jesus circumcised on the eighth day, and forty days after giving birth Mary subjected herself to the purification rituals required by the Law. (Leviticus 12:2-8) When Jesus was dedicated at the Temple, Simeon took Him in his arms and blessed Him, addressing Mary with these words: "Behold, this child is set for the fall and rising of many in Israel, and for the sign that is spoken against (and a sword will pierce through your own soul also), that thoughts out of many hearts may be revealed." (Luke 2:34-35) Simeon told Mary her child was no ordinary child; but a pivotal of faith. A faith when believed would gain and a faith when rejected would plummet. As Mary walked with her son, her soul would be pierced as she watched His sufferings.

Mary, Joseph and Jesus lived in Nazareth. However, Matthew 2:16-23 reports they escaped to Egypt for a time to avoid Herod's murderous rampage on children. Nazareth was located in the Galilean hills. On a clear day, a person could see approximately thirty miles. The large town of Sepphoris was some ten miles away.

Mary, the mother of Jesus Christ, was not excused from her duties as wife and mother. Her home was probably modest, constructed of unburned clay bricks, perhaps protected by stone-slab casings. The windows would have been high; the small bedrooms off the living space. Cooking was done on a hearth with the smoke escaping through the door or windows. There being no chimney. Food was served on a wooden platter set on the floor or a low table. Furniture was sparse consisting mostly of rugs, mats, pillows and clay lamps. The roof was overlaid with rafters, brushwood and mud. Stairs on the outside of the house led to the functional roof serving many purposes such as washing clothes, bathing, relaxing, drying fruit and vegetables, and a guest sleeping space. Joseph, Mary's husband, was a carpenter. (Matthew 13:55) He taught Jesus the carpentry trade. (Mark 6:3) The family spoke the Aramaic language, but would have had a working knowledge of Hebrew and Greek. It was in this environment, guided by Mary and Joseph, that Jesus grew in stature and wisdom. (Luke 2:40)

As was expected of Jews by the Law, Mary and Joseph went to Jerusalem to observe the Feast of Passover. When the feast was ended they left. People traveled in groups, so the fact Jesus was not with them was unnoticed until they had been traveling for almost a day. Mary and Joseph returned to Jerusalem to look for Jesus. When they found Him, He was in the temple sitting among the teachers, listening to them and asking questions. All who heard Him were amazed at His understanding and His answers. (Luke 2:46-47) Mary addressed Jesus and asked: "Why have you treated us so?" Jesus answered, "How is it that ye sought me? Wist ye not that I must be about my Father's business?" (Luke 2:49-52, KJV) Jesus went with His earthly parents and was subject to them. And He continued to increase in wisdom and stature and in favor with God and man. It was Mary, not Joseph, who disciplined her Son and kept a pondering heart full of things she did not fully understand.

We have little information about Mary and even less about Joseph after Jesus became an adult: "Joseph seems to have died comparatively early, for his name disappears from the narrative altogether." (*The Life and Teaching of Jesus*, p. 30.) We know Mary attended events where Jesus was present. (e.g. the wedding at Cana, John 2:1-11) She also exercised authority as Jesus' mother and showed remarkable insight about Jesus' power over nature. She knew, if He would, Jesus could produce wine out of water. Perhaps Mary witnessed Jesus' baptism, the descending dove and God saying "Thou art my beloved Son; with thee I am well pleased." (Luke 3:22) Maybe she knew when Jesus went into the wilderness to be tempted, or when He called His Disciples, calmed the sea, walked on water, healed the sick and cast out demons. As a matter of fact, she came once with Jesus' brothers to speak to Him or to seize Him because people said He was beside Himself. (Mark 3:21) Jesus took this opportunity to teach about the *eternal family*. (Mark 3: 31-35) Jesus was not a respecter of persons. His mission was to bring about the *eternal family*.

Mary was in the Upper Room where Jesus and His Disciples ate the *Last Supper* (Acts 1:14) Perhaps she was beside the road when Jesus rode into Jerusalem in triumph, in the crowd that cried *crucify Him* and at the court when Jesus was tried and condemned. She undoubtedly felt His pain at the cross. (John 19:25) Yes, Mary stood at the foot of the cross and listened to her Son's last words and watched Him die. Giving credence to the theory Joseph was already dead, at the cross Jesus asked John to take care of Mary. Jesus cared for His mother even from the cross.

So after Jesus was crucified, Mary went to live at John's house. (John 19:26-27) According to legend, John and Mary retired to Ephesus. Their presumed home lies a short distance from the archaeological precinct and can be visited even today.

Mary, the mother of Jesus, most blessed of all women was given a special place in the Bible. Mary's genealogy is traced back to Adam and Eve. (Luke 3:23-38, RSV) By linking Jesus' line with God's original creation, Luke shows Jesus' common humanity as contrasted with Matthew's emphasis on Jesus' royal heritage. (Matthew 1:1, RSV) Mary was told Jesus would be the seed of David. Mary was a descendant of David. (Acts 2:30; Romans 1:3; II Timothy 2:8) Old Covenant *proof texts* were used to persuade the early followers that Jesus was the Messiah. It was expected David would have a descendant on the throne. (Psalms 132:11-12)

Mary was the chosen vessel through which the Messiah came. The Catholic Church has exalted Mary. In the fifth century, the church began to think of Mary as a perpetual virgin. In 1854, the theory of the immaculate conception of Mary was embraced. In 1950, the pope declared the theory of the assumption of Mary; that her body did not decompose, but was reunited to her soul soon after death. (*Pictorial Bible Dictionary*, p. 515.) The Protestant Church believes Mary is honored above all women but that she was human and died just as all humans die.

ELIZABETH

Luke 1:5-41

Elizabeth was the second woman written about in the Bible who encountered and recognized Jesus. When Mary came to visit her, Elizabeth was filled with the Holy Spirit and "exclaimed with a loud cry, *Blessed are you among women, and blessed is the fruit of your womb! And, why is this granted me, that the mother of my Lord should come to me?*" (Luke 1:42-43)

Elizabeth was a Levite from the daughters of Aaron. She was married to Zechariah the priest. They lived in a city in the hill country of Southern Judaea. She was a righteous woman who had been unable to bear children. Women who were barren in that time felt God had looked on them with disfavor. An angel appeared to her husband and told him Elizabeth would conceive and they would have a son who would: "be great before the Lord and he shall drink no wine nor strong drink, and he will be filled with the Holy Spirit, even from his mother's womb. And he will turn many of the sons of Israel to the Lord their God, and he will go before him in the spirit and power of Elijah, to turn the hearts of the fathers to the children, and the disobedient to the wisdom of the just, to make ready for the Lord a people prepared." (Luke 1:15-17)

Elizabeth, in her old age, conceived and for five months hid herself. It was then believed God had lifted her reproach with the blessing of a child. Her child was not just any child, but the child who would herald the very Son of God, the Messiah. Elizabeth and Zechariah were instructed by the angel of the Lord to name him John. John the Baptist or Baptizer lived as a Nazarite in the desert. Some believe John spent some time with the Essenes, a very devout Jewish sect who lived separate from others and believed in the coming of two Messiahs. (*Pictorial Bible Dictionary*, p. 438) The Essenes also believed in resurrection. When he came forth as a prophet in about A.D. 26-27, John wore sack-cloth and ate locust and honey. He preached a baptism of repentance for the forgiveness of sins. (Luke 3:3) Luke quotes Isaiah 40:3-5 as a *proof text* for John the Baptizer's appearance on the scene. Elizabeth's son caused quite a stir. John told the people there was one coming that "is mightier than I, the thong of whose sandals I am not worthy to untie; he will baptize you with the Holy Spirit and with fire." (Luke 3:16) John's baptism was in preparation for the Messianic baptism.

John did in fact, at Jesus' request, baptize Jesus. Later, John said to some of the Disciples, "Behold the Lamb of God, which taketh away the sin of the world." (John 1:29)

John the Baptist was imprisoned and beheaded after speaking out against Herod's adulterous relationship with his brother's wife Herodias. Elizabeth must have suffered much as she watched her long awaited son fulfill his purpose in God's plan. Elizabeth was a woman of honor, chosen by God, to mother the child who was the forerunner of Jesus.

ANNA

Luke 2:36-38

Anna was a *one man woman* who must have loved and honored God with her marriage. Her name means *grace*. She was the daughter of Phanuel whose name means *face of God*. Names were given to describe individuals; therefore, we may infer that Anna came from a Godly family. She was from the relatively insignificant tribe of Asher. They were given the territory along the Mediterranean in the northwest corner of Palestine, known today as Acre. (Joshua 19:24-31) The town is located about 95 miles northwest of Jerusalem. Through the ages, Acre has been called by many names and many battles have been fought on its soil. The tribe of Asher dwelled among the Canaanites.

We are not told how or why Anna came to be in Jerusalem. She was married and widowed after only seven years of marriage. Her husband's name and origin is not given. She was a virgin when she married and never remarried. As far as we know, she had no children. Luke reports this prophetess was 84 years of age when she was found ministering in the temple. She did not depart from the temple, worshipping with fasting and prayer night and day. (Luke 2:37)

When Joseph and Mary brought Jesus to the temple to present Him to the Lord, Anna recognized Him as the Messiah and "spoke of Him to all who were looking for the redemption of Jerusalem." (Luke 2:38) Luke is the only Gospel writer who records the story of Anna.

> ## 21st Century Perspective
>
> **Jesus wasn't just any baby;
> He was God incarnate.
> We all want our babies to grow up and do great things—but think about it—Mary's baby became the Savior of the world! Is it any wonder that she kept things and *pondered them in her heart*?**

TO PONDER:

Read Proverbs 22:6 and think about the following:

❖ What is your earliest childhood memory?

❖ Who taught you about Jesus?

❖ When you were a child, was there anyone who blessed you and gave you encouragement? Who trained you?

❖ Do you know a widow who serves God? How? Who has she blessed? How?

Part One, Chapter Three, Lesson Twenty-Two

JESUS' MINISTRY OF HEALING AND COMPASSION (DEMONS)

JESUS' MINISTRY OF HEALING AND COMPASSION

At about age 30, Jesus reluctantly began His ministry of healing and compassion at the insistence of His mother at a wedding in Cana. The wedding host was running out of wine. Mary, Jesus' mother, insisted He provide wine for the party. She told the servants: *Do whatever He tells you . . .* Jesus said to them "Fill the jars with water. . . . Now draw some out and take it to the steward of the feast.

When the steward of the feast tasted the water now become wine . . . the steward called the bridegroom and said to him . . .you have kept the good wine until now." (John 2:1-11)

For the next three years Jesus traversed Palestine ministering to the needs of people and teaching about the coming of the Kingdom of God. Through Jesus, God was launching a New Covenant. In the past, God's laws were written on tablets of stone and God's presence was found in the tabernacle and temple. With the launching of the New Covenant, and the coming of the Holy Spirit, God's laws and presence would be found written on the hearts of people. And, people would worship God in spirit and truth.

Jesus showed no partiality of persons when it came to healing and compassion. While it was true He was first sent to *the lost sheep of Israel*, (Matthew 10:6; 15:24). He soon was confronted with the needs and faith of people from other nations and cultures. Demons, diseases and even death were subject to the authority of Jesus Christ. He made no difference between the Jew and Greek, male or female, slave or free. (Galatians 3:28) A person's status in life did not matter. Jesus had come to guide all people in the right way. He said, "I am the way, and the truth and the life, no one comes to the Father but by me." (John 14:6) When Jesus sent His Disciples out to minister in His Name, He gave them power to cast out demons, heal the sick and raise the dead. (Luke 9:1-2) Jesus' ministry of healing and compassion did not end with the end of His earthly ministry. Those who believe and are baptized have the power to carry on ministry in Jesus' name even today. (Mark 16:16-18)

MARY MAGDALENE

Matthew 27: 56-61; 28:1f; Mark 15:40-47; 16:1-9; Luke 8:2; 23:55; 24:10; John 19:25; 20:11-18

The name *Mary* is derived from the Hebrew *Miryam*. Magdalene indicates the area from which she came. Therefore, this Mary was most likely from the fishing town of Magdala which is located on the southwest coast of the Sea of Galilee 75-80 miles from Jerusalem.

We are not told how she made her living. Some believe she was the known sinner of Bethany who anointed Jesus' feet while He was eating dinner at the Pharisee's house. (*Jesus and Courageous Women*, p. 74) However, it is possible she was a different woman. She had seven demons before Jesus made her clean. Demons caused all kinds of situations from illnesses to super human intelligence and enormous physical strength. Seven was seen as a full or complete number. She must have been totally depraved. Perhaps she was a prostitute or maybe she practiced magic. The Scriptures simply do not tell us. Did she seek Jesus to fine relief like the servant girl in Acts 16:16-18? Or did Jesus have compassion on her and demand the demons depart from her as He did with the demonic man in Mark 5: 9-13?

Demons recognize Jesus and know He has power over them. In the case of the demonic man, Legion (the number of demons) spoke to Jesus and asked they be cast into a herd of swine. When the demons left the man, he was later found clothed and in his right mind, a condition that had not existed before he met Jesus.

How thankful Mary Magdalene must have been to be rid of those unclean spirits; so thankful, in fact that she became a devout follower of Jesus. Along with many other women, she followed Jesus as He traveled throughout the cities and villages in Galilee. (Matthew 4:23) She gave of her own means to provide for the needs of Jesus and the other Disciples. While some of the women who followed Jesus were married, there is no mention of Mary Magdalene's husband. She followed Jesus to Jerusalem, but did she know about His purpose? Was she prepared for His death and resurrection? Did she understand that His mission was to die on the cross for the sins of the world? Did any of the Disciples understand? John reported. Mary Magdalene, Mary the mother of Jesus, and Mary, wife of Clopas were by the cross when Jesus was crucified. Other sources place Mary Magdalene as watching from afar. It was dangerous for her to be near the cross. Often friends and family were killed when they became too involved or showed grief for a convicted criminal. Therefore, she showed a great deal of courage by being there. (*Jesus and Courageous Women*, p. 75.) She was not only at the cross, but she was also seen sitting across from the sepulcher, in the garden (Matthew 27:61) where Joseph of Arimathea placed Jesus' body for burial. (John 19:41)

On that Sunday, Mary Magdalene and some other women came before day-light to anoint Jesus' body with oil and spices. They wondered how they would remove the large heavy stone that had been placed over the door of the sepulcher; but to their surprise it had already been removed and the body of Jesus was gone. Mary assumed someone had taken the body. She ran and told Peter and John and they went to the tomb. All they found was Jesus' grave clothes. After Peter and John left, Mary Magdalene stood weeping outside the tomb. She stooped to look inside the tomb and saw two angels dressed in dazzling white sitting where Jesus' body had been. The angels asked her why she was weeping. She said "because they have taken away my Lord and I do not know where they have laid him." (John 20:13) Mary did not realize Jesus had been raised from the dead. She turned and saw a man whom she presumed to be the gardener and asked where he might have taken her Lord. But, then the man spoke, *"Mary,"* and she recognized His voice and replied in Hebrew, *"Rabboni"* which means *teacher*. It's easy to picture her running to Him and hugging Him. Her sorrow had turned to joy! Jesus told her "do not hold on to me for I have not yet ascended to my Father and your Father, My God and your God." (John 20: 17) Jesus elevated Mary to sisterhood with Him. They share the same Father and the same God. Mary Magdalene had the privilege of being the first Disciple to see and touch the resurrected Lord. All four Gospels report that Jesus appeared to Mary Magdalene first. Jesus told her to go and tell the brethren. Therefore, she went and told the other Disciples that she had seen and spoken with Jesus. (John 20:18) "As a result of Mary Magdalene's role as one sent (apostellein) by Jesus to witness to the male apostles . . . she was the only woman besides Jesus' mother on whose feast the creed was recited in the Western church. (*Jewish Antiquities*) Because of her mission to the apostles, Mary

Magdalene is often referred to as the *Apostle to the Apostles*. (*The Mass of the Roman Rite*, p. 470.) In *Jesus and Courageous Women*, p.78, Elsa Tamez considers Mary Magdalene to have been an Apostle: "She had all the necessary qualifications that are established by the church today for someone to be called an Apostle. She followed and was a part of the movement of Jesus in Galilee, and witnessed his death and resurrection." Perhaps Jesus considered her to be one of the elite. He certainly singled her out for a special blessing and for a very special place in the Gospel story.

THE SYROPHEONICIAN WOMAN

Matthew 15: 21-28; Mark 7: 26-30

A Greek speaking, Canaanite woman living in the ancient coastal region of Tyre had a daughter who was possessed by an unclean spirit or demon. Herodotus dates the founding of Tyre as early as 2740 B.C.. (*Pictorial Bible Dictionary*, p. 873) The woman would have lived with a rich multi-cultural tradition. She addressed Jesus as *the son of David*, therefore honoring the traditions of the Jews. She fell down at Jesus' feet, begging Him with humility and persistence to remove the demon from her daughter. There was no sign of offense when Jesus told her "Let the children first be fed, for it is not right to take the children's bread and throw it to the dogs." (Mark 7:27) She reasoned with Jesus that even the dogs were allowed to eat the children's crumbs. (Mark 7:28) Jesus had come first to the Jews, but even in the formative stage of the Jesus movement, He could not turn down a Gentile woman of great faith. Jesus healed the woman's daughter. When she returned home, she found her daughter lying in bed and the demon was gone. The woman's faith was like that of the centurion whose daughter was also healed without Jesus seeing or touching her.

Thirty years later, Paul went to the community of Tyre and found faithful believers there. (Acts 21:5) Could this faithful Gentile women have been *like a tree planted by streams of water that yields its fruit in its* season?" (Psalm 1:3)

21st Century Perspective

We live in a world today where the spiritual world of demons is especially intriguing.

Evil is alive and well.

As you pray the Lord's Prayer, remember you are asking to be delivered from evil.

TO PONDER:

Read Titus 3:3-7 and think about the following:

❖ What do you believe about demons?

❖ Is there evil present in your life? What?

❖ How can evil be eradicated from your life? From the community? From your country? From the world?

Part One, Chapter Four, Lesson Twenty-Three

JESUS' MINISTRY OF HEALING AND COMPASSION (DISEASE)

THE COVENANT WOMAN

THE UNCLEAN WOMAN

Matthew 9:20-22; Mark 5: 24-34; Leviticus 15: 19-30

According to the Law of Moses there are many things that could make a Jewish person *unclean*: childbirth, leprosy, fluids discharged from the body such as semen or blood, touching a cadaver, or touching an unclean person or any place or thing the unclean person touched. (Leviticus 15:25) There were also very strict cleansing rituals, and often the unclean person was made to live outside the community until the cleansing ritual was complete. When necessary the unclean person's clothes, house and things were burned.

With little medical knowledge and a culture teeming with magical lore and religious ritual, people relied mainly on the priest for relief from disease. The priest was clearly the most powerful person in the clan. Even in the first century when Jesus healed the lepers, He told them to go and show themselves to the priest. (Luke 17: 12-14)

The unnamed, unclean woman from the west bank of the Sea of Galilee was most likely pre-menopausal. She had her period for twelve years. This condition of continuous bleeding is often brought on by fibroid tumors in the womb encroaching upon the lining of the womb, depleting the body of blood so as to cause severe anemia. (*Pictorial Bible Dictionary*, p. 221) Twelve years of excessive bleeding would have undoubtedly brought on anemia. Common symptoms of anemia are "overall weakness, dizziness and fainting, heart palpitations, breathlessness, lack of libido, gastro-intestinal bleeding, ulcers, slow healing, fatigue, pallor, violent mood swings, irritability, and spots before the eyes. Secondary signs of deficient iron include apathy, brittle nails, poor appetite, hair loss, pale skin and lips, headaches and poor memory." (*Healthy Healing and Alternative Healing Reference*, p. 142.)

Picture this woman; sick and weak, desperate for relief. Aside from feeling sick all the time, she was socially and emotionally cast aside by her family, friends and the religious leaders of the synagogue. The illness was seen as having been brought on by some sin in her life. Her husband could not touch her; therefore, sex and children were out of the question. She could not worship God with other people because she could not enter the synagogue. Any place she entered would become defiled. (Leviticus 15:19-30) All her money was gone and perhaps her family's money as well. She had spent all she had on doctors. The priest and the medical practitioners of that day simply had no help for her.

When she heard Jesus was coming, she took a risk. She went into the crowd hoping to just touch the hem of Jesus' garment. Upon touching Jesus, she received power from Him. Jesus asked, "who touched Me?" (Mark 5:30) The Disciples thought He was crazy. They said in this crowd of people all pressing up against each other you asked *who touched you*? But, the woman knew exactly what Jesus was talking about. She came forward trembling and bowed before Jesus and told Him what she had done. Jesus told the woman her faith had made her well. For the first time in twelve years she was free from her disease.

This story holds much more meaning than just a woman being healed. Jesus demonstrated principles of the New Covenant. Jesus came to show the world a more perfect way. When the woman touched Jesus, he did not become unclean. Jesus included women in His ministry without discrimination. This woman openly defied the Jewish Law in order to receive healing. There are occasions when one must take a stand in order to change society for the better. Jesus called her *daughter* (Mark 5:34) including her in the family of God. A woman who was unclean and unaccepted met Jesus and became clean and accepted.

THE WOMAN WHO WORSHIPPED

Luke 13:10-18

Jesus had gone, as was His custom, to the synagogue. Perhaps He had been invited to teach there by the ruler of the synagogue. As Jesus was teaching, He saw a woman who was bent over and could not straighten herself. She had been in that condition for eighteen years. Apparently Jesus stopped in the middle of His message to relieve her suffering. (Luke 13:10 and Luke 13:18) He called to her and said, *woman, you are freed from your infirmity.* (Luke 13:12) And He laid His hands upon her and immediately she was made straight. She exalted God and proclaimed dignify and honor to God with intense joy. *And, she praised God.* (Luke 13:13) This was in direct contrast to the reaction of the ruler of the synagogue who became indignant and told the people they had six days to come to be healed; no work was to be done on the Sabbath.

The Synagogue attendant believed he obeyed the law. (Exodus 20:9-10). However, Jesus came to give a different perspective on the Sabbath. Jesus saw the actions of the officials at the synagogue as hypocritical. Did they not untie their cattle and take them for water on the Sabbath? This *daughter of Abraham* deserved more than an animal. She deserved to be loosed from her burden and brought to the *living water*.

Jesus also healed the man with the withered hand, (Matthew 12:11-12 and Luke 6:6) the man with dropsy, (Luke 14:1) a man at Bethzatha who couldn't walk (John 5:8-11) and the blind (John 9:14), all, on the Sabbath. Jesus stated that the Sabbath was made for man, not man for the Sabbath. (Mark 2:27) Jesus shamed His adversaries and brought joy to the people who came to worship.

While some sources teach that men and women worshipped on opposite sides of the synagogue, (Pictorial Bible Dictionary, p.818.), others teach that at the time of Jesus, men and women sat together. If this was the case this woman with the infirmity would have participated alongside men: "In Jesus' time, women participated fully in the religious life of the community. This included participation in synagogue services and in the regular study sessions that were conducted in the synagogue's *bet Midrash* (house of study). There was no separation of the sexes in synagogues and women could be counted as part of the required congregational quorum of ten adults. The idea that ten males are required for quorum is not found in ancient sources until at least 500 C.E. There was, however, one inequality. For social reasons, women were not allowed to read the Scriptures publicly." (*Jerusalem Perspective Article*: "The Place of Women in First-Century Synagogues", www.) The order of service would have been as follows:

❖ "Two thanksgivings, one being: *Blessed art thou, O Lord our God, king of the world, former of light and creator of darkness, author of peace and creator of all things.*

❖ The Shema: *Hear, O Israel, the Lord our God, the Lord is One, and thou shall love the Lord thy God with all thy heart and with all thy soul, and with all thy might* (Deuteronomy 6: 4)

- ❖ Prayer: any adult male from the congregation

- ❖ Scripture lesson from the Pentateuch (perhaps the Decalogue)

- ❖ A lesson from the Prophets

- ❖ Sermon or exhortation: Jesus on many occasions gave this part of the service. (Matthew 4:23, Mark 1:21 and 6:2; Luke 4:15, 16, 17, 20, 6:6 and 13:10; John 6:59 and 18:20; Acts 13:15, 16)

- ❖ Closing: A blessing which had to be pronounced by a priest and the congregation responded with an *Amen*. If no priest was present a prayer was offered." (*Pictorial Bible Dictionary*, p. 819.

Toward the end of the first century, eighteen prayers were added to the worship service, which were *recited every morning, afternoon and evening*. (*Holeman Bible Handbook*, p. 525.) While women, for cultural reasons, were exempt from many of the worship rituals, they were not exempt from the *Eighteen Benedictions*. One wonders how the *Eighteen Benedictions* evolved. Could it have had its roots in the infirmities of this *daughter of Abraham* who had suffered for 18 years, but found relief and salvation through the blessings of Jesus?

> ### 21st Century Perspective
>
> **Jesus not only touched unclean women and healed them of diseases for which doctors had no cure, He gave gifts to His Disciples enabling them to do the same. There are many healers today, from those doing healing touch to surgeons and all of them may be called of God. Faith healing is also among the gifts from God. Jesus said,** *Take heart, daughter; your faith has made you well."*
> **Matthew 9:22**

TO PONDER:

Read James 5:16 and I Peter 2:24 and think about the following:

- ❖ Where is healing needed in your life? Physical? Emotional? Spiritual? Social?

- ❖ Do you want to be healed? What would be different if you were healed? What would you have to give up? What would you gain?

- ❖ What steps do you need to take in order to be healed?

Part One, Chapter Five, Lesson Twenty-Four

JESUS' MINISTRY OF HEALING AND COMPASSION (DEATH)

THE COVENANT WOMAN

JAIRUS' DAUGHTER

Luke 8: 40-56; Matthew 9:18-26; Mark 5:21-43

It appears that Jairus's daughter was a teenager. Few teenagers are mentioned in the Bible. It has been said only Western culture has the *rebellious teenager*. It appears children in the first century made the transition from childhood to adulthood in a more relaxed manner than children in the twenty-first century. However, at age twelve, after the Passover Feast, Jesus may have seemed rebellious when He stayed behind to *be about His Father's business*. (Luke 2:42-52) At age twelve a Jewish boy became a *son of the law* and was then regarded as a religious adult. Women were also included. Males were required to attend the religious feast. Women were not required to attend, but they could and often did attend the feast. Adolescent girls were also considered to be young adults. They took on the duties and responsibilities of women and were often married at an early age. It is significant that Jairus' daughter is the only twelve year old mentioned in the New Covenant other than Jesus Himself.

The Bible tells us more about her father than about the girl. Jarius was an official of the Synagogue, possibly a *lay president* chosen to preside over the services and business. (*Jesus-The Man, The Mission, And The Message*, p. 274.) He would have planned the order of service and guest speakers. (Acts 13:15) This was obviously a family of distinction, a family that was well known in the area.

Jesus had returned from a trip across the Sea of Galilee to the west bank. The large crowd was excited about the prospects of seeing Jesus. Perhaps Jairus was a follower of Jesus or perhaps he had just become desperate enough to ask for Jesus' help. The followers of Jesus had not yet become a separate group apart from the Jews. Regardless of why he came to Jesus, it was his faith and not his daughter's that made her live. He bowed down before Jesus, asking that Jesus come and restore health to a daughter who was near death. Jesus began the trip to Jarius' home, but was delayed when He stopped to heal a woman. Perhaps the delay occurred in order that a more profound miracle could be demonstrated. Likewise, Jesus was also delayed when he was asked to come to the side of Lazarus. This event also became a resurrection instead of a healing. (John 11:1-45) Word came that they should no longer bother: the girl was dead. But, Jesus said *not so, she was only asleep*. Perhaps He meant she was in a coma or perhaps He used the familiar term *sleep* for death because He knew He could bring her back to life. Rabbis of that time *held that God raised the dead through the instrumentality of righteous men* (*Jesus-The Man, The Mission, And The Message*, p. 275.). In the Old Covenant, Elijah and Elisha were credited with being instruments of righteousness. Both were used to bring the dead back to life. (I Kings 17:17-24 and II Kings 4: 32-37)

The crowd was not allowed to accompany Jesus into the house. The entire crowd was put aside for Jesus to be present with this one young lady. Jesus told Jairus, *Be not afraid, only believe*. (Mark 5:36; Luke 8:50) Her mother, her father, Peter, James and John were the chosen few to witness this miracle. Jesus spoke, *"Tal'itha Cu'mi* which means little girl, I say to you rise". (Mark 5: 41) Her spirit returned to her and she got up and walked. She was then given something to eat. This was a testimony that she was really alive. People who are alive walk and eat. The resurrected Lazarus had dinner with his family and Jesus. (John 12:2) Jesus also walked, talked and ate after He was raised from the dead. He even made breakfast for his Disciples. (John 21:4-14) The *little girl's* parents were amazed! She, too, must have been amazed, raised by the Father, able to walk and eat and to once again bring joy to her family.

THE WIDOW OF NAIN

Luke 7:11-17

This woman lived in the beautiful city of Nain, which was traversed with a broad view of valleys and mountains. She was a widow whose only son had died. He appears to have been a young adult. Her son would have been her provider and protector. In Luke 7:13 it is said Jesus had compassion on her and raised her son from the dead. She and her son must have been well known in the city; for Luke 7:12 reports, *a large crowd from the city was* with *her.*

Apparently the woman did not reach out to Jesus or attempt to win His favor. She did nothing to deserve Jesus' compassion. Likewise, her son had done nothing to merit Jesus' attention. But because Jesus had compassion on her, and raised her son, the news of Jesus' miracles spread through Judea and the surrounding countryside. (Luke 7:17)

> ### 21st Century Perspective
>
> **Jesus raised people from the dead and was Himself raised from the dead in order that we may believe in the resurrection of the dead.** *Our commonwealth is in heaven and from it we await a Savior, the Lord Jesus Christ, who will change our lowly body to be like his glorious body, by the power which enables him even to subject all things to himself.*
> **Philippians 3:20-21**

TO PONDER:

Read John 14:2 and 14:19 and think about the following:

- ❖ What do you believe about life after death?

- ❖ Are you afraid of death? Why?

- ❖ Jesus has prepared a place for you. Have you prepared to accept that gift from Him?

Part One, Chapter Six, Lesson Twenty-Five

WOMEN WHO MINISTERED WITH JESUS

WOMEN WHO MINISTERED WITH JESUS

Jesus ministered throughout Judah, Samara and Galilee. Wherever He went, crowds of people came to hear His words, be healed and to receive forgiveness for their sins. It is specifically pointed out women contributed in many different ways to His ministry. (Luke 8:2-3) They provided their homes for lodging, rest, meals and fellowship. (Luke 10:38) Women acted as evangelists to tell others about Jesus and supported their husbands, sons and daughters who worked in Jesus' ministry. At least one woman served as a conduit to warn her husband about Jesus' righteousness. (Matthew 27:19) They gave of their means to support Jesus' ministry. (Luke 8:3) Women supported Jesus in word and deed, lamenting His imminent death, anointing His body for burial, standing by Him at the cross and remaining faithful to Jesus through a ministry of presence until His ascension and beyond. "The early Christians thought of and referred to the women who are mentioned as Disciples." (*New Testament Apocrypha*, Vol. 1, p. 246.) Jesus' disciples are no different in the 21st century. Women still minister with Jesus.

MARTHA

Luke 10: 38-41; John 11: 1-39; 12:2

There are many references in the Bible which place Jesus in Bethany, a small town approximately two miles from Jerusalem (Matthew 26: 6-13, Mark 14: 3-9, Matthew 21: 17, Mark 11: 1-11, John 1: 28, John 11: 1f, John 12: 1-8). John 1:28 identifies Bethany as being beyond the Jordan in Judea. "Today [Bethany] is believed to be the city of El-Azarijeh. This city contains the supposed tomb of Lazarus and the house of Simon the leper." (*Pictorial Bible Dictionary*, p. 108) Could it be the house of Simon the leper is also the house of Simon the Pharisee? When Jesus was in Bethany at the house of Simon the leper, a woman anointed his head with an alabaster flask of nard. (Matthew 26:6-12, Mark 14: 3-9) In Luke 7:36-50, Simon the Pharisee asks Jesus to come to his house for dinner. The main meal of the day was usually served at sundown. As they were eating a woman came with an alabaster flask of ointment, wet Jesus feet with her tears, wiped them with her hair, kissed and anointed them. At this time, Jesus addressed the Pharisee by the name of Simon. Another example was reported in Bethany as Jesus and the newly resurrected Lazarus were eating supper, Mary, the sister of Martha, took pure nard and anointed Jesus' feet and wiped His feet with her hair. Perhaps Mary had performed this ritual for Jesus before as an act of worship.

It is quite possible Martha was a relative of, possibly the widow of, Simon the Leper. (*Pictorial Bible Dictionary*, pp. 513-514; Matthew 26:6-12, Mark 14:3) As a widow, Martha would have been in charge of her house and would have had privileges a married woman might not have had. First Timothy 5:1-16 speaks about widows. The notes accompanying this passage inform us: "three classes of widows are mentioned: (a) real widows are older women who depend upon the church for support (Acts 6:1); (b) enrolled widows are Christian workers whose qualifications are detailed; they pledge themselves to the service of Christ; (c) younger widows are encouraged to remarry."

While these standards were endorsed in early church times, they would have been taken from existing norms and could have applied to Martha and other widows of her time. Martha would have fallen into the second category. She was apparently very active and managed her house well. She can be pictured as a woman between fifty and sixty years of age who has her younger siblings living in her house. Perhaps Lazarus and Mary worked to support the family while Martha managed the home. In that time, "urban women had freedom to engage in social and business affairs." (*Holman Bible Handbook*, p. 357.) Jesus was invited, not to Mary's or Lazarus' home, but to Martha's home. Martha received the guest. (Luke 10:38-42) It was usually the man of the house who received the guest. This custom went back as far as Abraham. (Genesis 18:1-8)

Jesus was close to this family: "Jesus loved Martha, Mary and Lazarus." (John 11:5) And it appears He spent a great deal of time with them. (Matthew 21:17; Mark 11:1, 11) On one occasion Martha became anxious because she had much housework to do and her sister, Mary, was sitting at the feet of Jesus listening to Him teach. Martha asked Jesus to make Mary help her with the chores. Jesus said that Mary had chosen the better thing to do and He would not take that away from her. Martha could have prepared a simple meal, but apparently she felt the need for more. Some foods she may have prepared are as follows: bread-the foundation food, vegetables such as coosa (squash), rice, cabbage, beans, lentils, onions and seasonal fruits, such as oranges, lemons, pomegranates, apricots, plums, figs and grapes. Cheese and curds were common; fish and meat were served on special occasions. People usually drank water or wine. Meal preparation was no easy task. There were no packaged or prepared foods. Fixing a meal for fifteen or more people would have taken a major effort. Martha's anxiety may have prompted a later lesson Jesus taught to His Disciples: He said, "Therefore I tell you, do not be anxious about your life, what you shall eat, nor about your body, what you shall put on. For life is more than food, and the body more than clothing." He goes on to say God feeds the birds, grows the flowers, and God's people will be cared for when they seek His kingdom. (Luke 12:22-32)

While Martha was burdened with household chores, she did not neglect her relationship with Jesus. They were obviously close. She was familiar enough with Jesus to complain to Him about Mary not helping her. She knew she could rely on Jesus for help. When Lazarus got sick, she and Mary sent word to Jesus. But Jesus said, "This illness is not unto death; it is for the glory of God, so that the Son of God may be glorified by means of it." (John 11:4) So Jesus waited for two days. When He arrived near the village where Martha lived, Lazarus had been in the grave for four days. When Martha heard Jesus had arrived, she went out to meet Him. The following conversation took place: "Martha said to Jesus, *Lord, if you had been here, my brother would not have died. And even now I know that whatever you ask from God, God will give you.* Jesus said to her, *your brother will rise again.* Martha said to him, *I know that he will rise again in the resurrection at the last day.* Jesus said to her, *I am the resurrection and the life; he who believes in me, though he die, yet shall he live, and whoever lives and believes in me shall never die. Do you believe this?* She said to him, *Yes, Lord; I believe that you are the Christ, the Son of God, he who is coming into the world.*" (John 11:21-27)

Martha's confession of faith is similar to Peter's confession of faith: "Now when Jesus came into the district of Caesarea Phillippi, he asked his Disciples, *who do men say that the Son of man is?* And, they said, *Some say John the Baptist, others say Elijah, and others Jeremiah or one of the prophets.* He said to them, *But who do you say that I am?* Simon Peter replied, You are *the Christ, the Son of the living God.* And Jesus answered him, *Blessed are you, Simon Bar-Jona! For flesh and blood has not revealed this to you, but my Father who is in heaven.*" (Matthew 16:13-17, Luke 9:18-20)

Jesus, Martha, Mary and the Jews who had come to comfort the family went to the tomb where Lazarus had been buried. Jesus told them to remove the stone from the door. Martha objected saying there would be an odor because the body had been dead for four days. Jesus reminded Martha, "Did I not tell you that if you would believe you would see the glory of God?" (John 11:40) Jesus called Lazarus from the grave to live again! And, six days before the Passover Lazarus and Jesus were found at the table eating the food Martha had prepared giving testimony to the fact he was alive and well. Lazarus and Jesus enjoyed the fruits of Martha's labor and hospitality as she continued to serve her Lord.

MARY

Luke 10: 38f; Matthew 26: 6-13; Mark 14: 3-9; John 11 and 12

When Jesus visited the home of Martha near Bethany, among those present was a young woman by the name of Mary. Mary was the sister of Martha and Lazarus. Apparently she lived with them in Bethany. There is no mention of her husband. One can picture Mary: slender, olive skin, very long black hair, dark knowing eyes with an expression of eagerness on her face as she sat at the feet of Jesus looking up into His face hanging on to His every word. It was not always acceptable for women to learn at the feet of a teacher in first-century Palestine. Women were expected to manage the home, and some poor women worked outside the home to help the family. Teachers usually sat in a higher, exalted position so their students could see, hear and show respect. In the first century students often sat on the floor at the feet of the teacher.

Jesus stood up to read at the synagogue in Nazareth. (Luke 4:16-17) Luke, the author of Acts, tells us the Apostle Paul was schooled at the feet of a well-known first-century educator by the name of Gamaliel. He was highly respected by the Pharisees and believed in the sovereignty of God. He once persuaded the people to allow Peter and John to continue their ministry in the infant church with the following speech: "So in the present case I tell you, keep away from these men and let them alone; for if this plan or this undertaking is of men, it will fail; but if it is of God, you will not be able to overthrow them. You might even be found opposing God!" (Acts 5:38-39)

Teachers were used by God to change circumstances that would bring about God's purpose. Jesus, the Teacher, changed the world: Paul later said of Jesus, "the pre-existent Christ became incarnate at a time determined by God in order to ransom those who were in bondage under the law." (Galatians 3:28-4:7, and notes, RSV) In the Old Covenant everyone, including females, was to learn to fear the Lord and obey His commandments. (Deuteronomy 31:12) Jesus loved the Old Covenant law, but he peeled away the superficial outer layer of the law and exposed the heart of the Law. God intended for males and females to be equal in knowledge and service. He refused to allow Martha to persuade Mary back into the *house maid* role. Jesus said Mary had chosen the better way. (Luke 10:42) Later as Jesus was teaching among the crowd a woman shouted to Jesus, "blessed is the womb that bore you, and the breast that you sucked! But he said, *Blessed rather are those who hear the word of God and keep it!*" (Luke 11:27-28) Women were not to be just good mothers, but also hearers of the word and keepers of the word of God.

When Lazarus died many Jews went to mourn his death. It was dangerous for Jesus to go to Bethany because the Jews around Jerusalem were seeking to kill him. (John 11: 8) When Jesus arrived in the area, Martha went out to meet Him while Mary stayed in the house with their guest. Perhaps she was helping with *crowd control* on Jesus' behalf. Later, Martha called Mary and she went outside the village to meet Jesus. The Jews thought Mary was going to the tomb to weep. When Mary saw Jesus, she fell at His feet. She said to Jesus: *Lord, if you had been here my brother would not have died.* (John 11:32) Mary was weeping. Jesus wept with her. And, then Jesus went to the tomb and called Lazarus to come forth. Mary and the others witnessed the miracle of resurrection. Many of the Jews who came to console Mary now believed the Messiah had come! Others incited the Pharisees who became more intent on finding and killing Jesus. Therefore, Jesus no longer went about openly among the Jews. (John 11:45-54)

At a supper in Bethany, Mary performed the act of a servant by washing Jesus' feet. She wiped His feet with her hair and anointed them with a pound of very expensive ointment called *nard*. Perhaps Mary had performed this service and act of worship for Jesus on other occasions (i.e. at Simon the Pharisee's house or Simon the Leper's house). There is no proof of who these men were or who the woman was who anointed Jesus. Mary was certainly devoted to Jesus. People at this gathering complained, as they did in the former examples: the ointment should have been sold and the money given to the poor. But Jesus said Mary had anointed His body in preparation for His burial. Perhaps Mary had heard well what Jesus was really teaching about his journey to the cross. Jesus had not only spoken the words of new life but had demonstrated the reality of new life through the raising of Lazarus. Perhaps Mary understood the full meaning of both the agony and the power of what Jesus' death and resurrection would bring.

WALKING WITH JESUS

JOANNA

Luke 8:3; Luke 24: 10

Joanna followed Jesus. We are not told of how she came to be involved in the Jesus movement, but we do know she was a faithful Disciple. She was among the women who gave of their own means to support Jesus' ministry as they traveled throughout the region of Galilee. She was married to a man named Chuza who was an employee of Herod Antipas. As a steward or overseer for the Tetrarch of Galilee, it is believed that *Chuza was undoubtedly a man of rank and means. (Pictorial Bible Dictionary*, p. 171) Perhaps Chuza supplied the funds for Joanna as she traveled with Jesus. Chuza and Joanna may have made their home on the grounds of the palace compound which was located in the walled city of Tiberias on the western shore of the Sea of Galilee: "The site included a palace, a forum, and a great synagogue." (*Pictorial Bible Dictionary*, p. 852) Perhaps Joanna had worshipped at the synagogue and may have heard Jesus speak there since Jesus often went to a synagogue to speak to the people. (Matthew 4:23)

Herod had his hands full managing his personal and political life. He had taken Herodias who was his half brother's wife. John the Baptist warned Herod and Herodias about their sin. Herodias decided to take revenge and manipulated the situation in order to have John the Baptist beheaded. The position of Tetrach was a relatively minor position, and Herod's cunning balancing act between the Jews and the Romans would soon come to an end. The beheading of John the Baptist began his final demise. He and Herodias eventually went into exile. As did many of the Jews, Herod most likely believed the Jesus movement was just another Jewish sect to be managed and exploited.

Therefore, he ignored the fact that people who worked for him were also working for the cause of Jesus. One wonders if Herod ever noticed his steward's wife was supporting the very man he would help crucify.

In any case, Joanna was not deterred, from following Jesus. She was with Mary Magdalene, Mary, the mother of James and other women on Friday when Jesus was crucified and buried and again on Sunday when Jesus was resurrected. The Bible says they obeyed the commandment to rest on Saturday, their Sabbath. (Luke 23:56) Sunday morning when the women came to anoint Jesus' body with spices she witnessed the angels who reminded her of what Jesus had told her and the others: "the Son of man must be delivered into the hands of sinful men, and be crucified, and on the third day rise." (Luke 24:7)The women went and told the Apostles, but the Apostles were not ready to believe. How privileged Joanna was to have been among the first to receive the message of Jesus' resurrection!

SUSANNA

Luke 8:3

Little is recorded about Susanna except she was a follower of Jesus and one of the women who provided for the ministry of Jesus out of her own means. (Luke 8:1-3) She was possibly one of the women Jesus healed from an infirmity or an unclean spirit. Scripture tells us that among the people who traveled with Him there were *some women who had been healed of evil* spirits *and infirmities*. (Luke 8:2) Perhaps she stood at a distance with other people who knew Jesus during the crucifixion, hearing Jesus forgive the thief on the cross. No doubt, she knew first-hand what it meant to be included in Jesus' ministry.

Her name is Shoshannah in Hebrew and Lily in Greek. The name means *a glowing red flower* and is a symbol of loveliness. It's possible she was a lovely Jewish woman, poised and intelligent.

By chance, Susanna's parents may have read the second to first century B.C. story about a lady of honor named Susanna. This story is included in the Apocrypha. The story goes something like this: Two lustful elders accused Susanna of having an affair with a young man. Daniel came to her defense, interrogated the elders and caught them in a lie. Therefore, Susanna was found innocent and "Hilkiah and his wife praised God for their daughter Susanna, and so did Joakim her husband and all her kindred because nothing shameful was found in her." (Susanna 1:63) Certainly this Susanna would have been a good role model for all future Susannas. She may give us some insight into the first-century woman who gave of herself and her means in order to serve the Lord.

SIMON PETER'S WIFE

Matthew 8:14; Mark 1:30; Luke 4:38; I Corinthians 9:5

The Bible barely alludes to this woman. Being the wife of Simon Peter must have been a wild ride. Peter, the Apostle, was out-spoken, impetuous and conceited. He was also one of the chosen three who was a part of the inner circle of Jesus. Simon Peter stepped out with his body and mouth. He tried to walk on water, cut off a servant's ear who came to take Jesus away, declared he would never desert Jesus, and then went on to deny Him three times in one night. However, he was also the first Disciple to confess Jesus as the Messiah and declared his love for Jesus three times. Peter means *rock* or *pebble*. When Simon Peter made his declaration of faith, Jesus said "Upon this rock I will build my church". (Matthew 16:15-18)

Peter seems to have preached to the Jews of the dispersion in Pontus, Galatia, Bithynia, Cappadocia and Asia and, at the end of his ministry, in Rome. (*Evangelism in the Early Church*, p. 167) Perhaps Peter's wife went with him and traveled as they proclaimed the Gospel together. Paul said, "Do we not have the right to be accompanied by a wife, as the other apostles and the brothers of the Lord and Cephas?" (I Corinthians 9:5) We know Peter and his wife had a house in Capernaum on the northwest shore of Galilee where her mother was either living with them or visiting. She was sick with a fever when Jesus went there. He healed her and she immediately got out of bed and served them. This was the second reported miracle of healing Jesus performed. Being a good Jew, Peter's wife would have cared for her mother. (Exodus 20:12, Leviticus 19: 3, Deuteronomy 5:16) Jesus did many miracles in Capernaum, but the city did not repent. In Matthew 11:23-24 and Luke 10:15 Jesus predicted the destruction of Capernaum. Today, the exact location can no longer be identified.

So Peter's wife lived in a city that was unrepentant, with a profoundly religious husband whose best friend was Jesus. We know her mother either lived with her or visited. She is certainly among the wives Peter wrote about in I Peter 3:1-6: "Likewise you wives, be submissive to your husbands, so that some though they do not obey the word, may be won without a word by the behavior of their wives, when they see your reverent and chaste behavior. Let not yours be the outward adorning with braiding of hair, decoration of gold, and wearing of fine clothing, but let it be the hidden person of the heart with the imperishable jewel of a gentle and quiet spirit, which in God's sight is very precious. So once the holy women who hoped in God used to adorn themselves and were submissive to their husbands, as Sarah obeyed Abraham, calling him Lord. And you are now her children if you do right and let nothing terrify you."

While the Bible does not mention her name, "tradition has it that her name was Concordia or Perpetua, that she suffered Martyrdom in Rome along with Peter and that Peter encouraged her by saying *remember, dear our Lord.*" (*Halley's Bible Handbook*, p. 606.) Perhaps she was in Rome with Peter and witnessed Peter's martyrdom as he was crucified upside down by Nero. (*Contemporary Thinking About Paul*, pp. 171-172.) She may have been the woman who sent greetings to the Christians in Asia Minor from Rome. (I Peter 5:13)

It would have taken a strong woman called of God to have been the wife of Simon Peter.

LAMENTING WOMEN

Luke 23: 27-31; Jeremiah 9: 17-22

Crucifixion was practiced by the Romans since the third century B.C. It was reserved for rebels, slaves and criminals of the lowest classes. The scene was highly emotional. Jesus had been tried, convicted, beaten and ridiculed. (Mark 15) He was carrying His own cross as he climbed the steeps to Golgotha (John 19:17) until Simon of Cyrene was compelled to carry the cross for Him. (Luke 23:26) Luke reported there were women in the crowd who had followed Jesus bewailing and lamenting for the man who was about to experience the cross. Perhaps these women were professional mourners or perhaps they were ordinary Disciples who truly mourned the impending loss of their leader. Professional mourning in first-century Jerusalem was a refined art form. Women were trained for the task.

The Covenant Woman

The prophet, Jeremiah, was a lamenter and is credited with having written the book of Lamentations in the Bible. (Introduction: The Lamentations of Jeremiah, RSV) He spoke of calling the skillful women to come and mourn. (Jeremiah 9:17) He said in Jeremiah 9:20, "Hear, O women, the words of the Lord, and let your ear receive the word of his mouth: teach to your daughters a lament and each to her neighbor a dirge."

Often a death in a family would bring on elaborate mourning bordering on hysteria lasting as long as a week or more. (*Pictorial Bible Dictionary*, p. 561) In the case of Jairus' daughter, the mourners were already gathered when Jesus arrived to bring her back from the dead. (Matthew 9:23; Mark 5:38) Mourners and people who came to console were also at Martha and Mary's home when Lazarus died. (John 11:19)

Because Jesus was tried so quickly and crucified in disgrace, there was no family gathering and likely no prearranged mourners. Those who bewailed and lamented on the way to Golgotha showed a lack of understanding for the events that were taking place. Jesus was not being taken from them. He was bringing about the New Covenant and obeying the will of His Father in order that everyone, henceforth, might experience His presence. Jesus turned to the women and said, "Daughters of Jerusalem, do not weep for me, but weep for yourselves and for your children. For behold, the days are coming when they will say, *Blessed are the barren, and the wombs that never bore, and the breast that never gave suck!*" (Luke 23:28-29) Jesus was centered in the will of God and did not need the laments of the women. His mission was about to be finished. (John 19:30) But, the people of Jerusalem would have a long hard task before them. Jesus understood it would not be easy for the early Christians.

PILATE'S WIFE

Matthew 27:19-26; Mark 15: 1-5; Luke 23:1,3; John 18:28-38; Acts 4: 27; 13: 13 ,28, 58; I Timothy 6:13; II Timothy 4:21

The *first lady* of Judea was an aloof woman of considerable influence. If rumors speak to us, she possibly could have been the Claudia mentioned in II Timothy 4:21. Others believe her name to have been Procle. (*Gospel of Nichodemus*, Part 1, chapter 4) The Bible does not give her a name. She was married to the ruthless Pontius Pilate who was the governor of Judea, Samaria and Old Idumea from A. D. 26-36. Pilate was the last Roman official to try Jesus.

Charlotte Bronte in her poem *Pilate's Wife's Dream* calls him an *unjust judge of destiny*. And, indeed he was. He did not hesitate to kill Galileans even as they sacrificed animals to God in worship. (Luke 13:1) Pilate was harsh with his subjects, and they frequently complained to Rome about him. (*Pictorial Bible Dictionary*, p. 657) So, what made Pilate hesitant to sacrifice another Galilean? Matthew 27:19 tells us "while he was sitting on the judgment seat, his wife sent word to him, *have nothing to do with that righteous man, for I have suffered much over him today in a dream.*" Was Pilate's wife a righteous woman? Apparently, during the night while Jesus was being sent from official to official to be condemned, God spoke to her in a dream. What kind of influence did Pilate's wife have over Pilate? Perhaps he sought to release Jesus because of his wife's warning. The Gospel writers portray Pilate as a weak man who feared the powerful Jews for political reasons. At any rate, when Pilate wanted to let Jesus go, the Jews cried out, "If you release this man, you are not Caesar's friend; every one who makes himself a king sets himself against Caesar." (John 19:12)

It was about noon when Pilate handed Jesus over to be crucified. He said "shall I crucify your king?" The chief priest answered "we have no king but Caesar." (John 19:15-16) Later when the title *Jesus of Nazareth, King of the Jews* was displayed over the cross, the chief priest objected, "do not write, *The King of the Jews*, but *This man said, I am King of the Jews*." Pilate answered. "What I have written I have written." (John 19:21-22) As Pilate washed his hands symbolizing his innocence for the condemnation of the innocent Jesus, one can surmise his wife's words were heavy on his mind. (Matthew 27:24)

The early church exonerated Pilate and his wife: "In the Abyssinian church, Pilate was canonized as a saint for his insistence on Jesus' innocence, and his wife was made a saint in the Greek Church because of her dream." (*Jesus, The Man, The Mission and the Message*, pp. 384-385) However, some believe the early Christians were too eager to accuse the Jews of killing Jesus. Is this the reason Pilate and his wife found favor in the Gospels and in the early church? Or did Pilate's repeated contact with Jesus have a profound impact on his and his wife's life? Perhaps both of them became Disciples of Christ as the early church history implies.

THE OTHER MARY

Matthew 27:56, 61; 28:1; Mark 15:47; 16:1, 8; Luke 8:2, 3; 24:10

There appears to have been several Marys associated with Jesus. However, three of them are consistently present: Mary the mother of Jesus, Mary Magdalene and Mary the mother of James the younger, and Joses [perhaps Joseph of Arimathea] are seen as significant in the Gospels. (Mark 15:40-41, Luke 24:10, Matthew 27:56) (*Jesus, The Man, The Mission, The Message*, p. 394.) The Scriptures identify James as an Apostle, the son of Alphaeus or Cleopas. People in the Bible are often known by Hebrew and Greek names. (John 19:25, Mark 15:42) Mary, then, would have been the wife of Alphaeus or Cleopas. Joseph of Arimathea was the man who asked for Jesus' body, brought spices, anointed the body for burial and buried Him. (John 19:39-40) It is possible the other Mary was from Arimathea. While scholars are uncertain about the exact location of Arimathea, it is believed to have been the *Ramah of Samuel's residence, in the hill-country of Ephraim about 20 miles NW of Jerusalem. (Pictorial Bible Dictionary*, p. 70.; I Samuel 1:1.) This would have been within the area of Jesus' Galilean ministry. By all indications, Mary had been one of Jesus' Disciples while He ministered in Galilee. She ultimately followed Him to Jerusalem, witnessed the crucifixion and was present when Jesus was buried. Perhaps the burial site was familiar to her, even a family burial place. In that time, families buried their dead in the same tomb. However, this place was newly hewn and had not been used. New tombs were reserved for people of honor. The tomb was fitting for the *King of the Jews*, the incarnate God.

The other Mary, Mary Magdalene, and Salome went very early in the morning on Sunday to anoint Jesus' body. (Luke 24:8-10) When they arrived, the stone slab to the entrance of the tomb had been rolled back. Jesus was not there. The women were excited and afraid. Where was Jesus? Had someone taken His body? One or perhaps two angels appeared and reminded the women about what Jesus had taught them. He told them, "the Son of man must suffer many things and be rejected by the elders and chief priest and scribes and be killed, and on the third day be raised." (Luke 9:18-22, 44; 17:25; 18: 31-34; Mark 9:30-32)

The Gospel of Mark was written first. The most ancient manuscripts end Mark with the women afraid and silent. However, the other Gospels report the women spoke to the angels and went to tell the male Disciples. (Matthew 28:8; Luke 24:9, 11, 22, 24; John 20:1-10)

The other Mary appears to have been a faithful follower of Jesus who set an example for her family as she actively participated in ministry with and for the Messiah.

SALOME

Matthew 20:20-21; 27:56; Mark 15:40-41; 16:1

The name Salome is the feminine form of Solomon which means *peaceable*. When her parents named her, they must have had great hopes for her future as they remembered the wise king from their past.

It appears Salome was the sister of Mary, the mother of Jesus. (Mark 27:56; John 19:25) She would have been a cousin to Elizabeth, the mother of John the Baptist, and indeed there is evidence the family followed John's teachings before they embraced Jesus as the Messiah. (John 1:35-39) Salome married Zebedee and they had at least two sons: James and John. James was the older. The family operated a fishing business. They were of the employer class, had servants and were acquainted with people of high standing as evidenced by John having known the high priest well enough to gain entrance for Peter and himself to the trial of Jesus. (John 18:16) Salome was able to contribute to Jesus' ministry with her own money and service as she traveled with Him in Galilee. Salome and Zebedee made their home possibly in Bethsaida in Galilee.

There is no doubt Salome was a close Disciple of Jesus. She was Jesus' aunt and familiar enough with Him to ask for a favor. She asked Jesus if her sons, James and John, could have first and second places of honor in His kingdom. (Matthew 20:20-21) Jesus explained these places were not His to give. That authority belonged to the Father alone. Did the request show Salome's knowledge of the heavenly kingdom or was she, like so many in that time, thinking Jesus would establish an earthly kingdom? Apparently, the other disciples thought James and John put their mother up to asking Jesus for the favor. Although Jesus could not grant her request, James and John were favored. They were privileged to be in the inner circle with Jesus. They witnessed the resurrection of Jairus' daughter. (Mark 5:37) Jesus took them with him to the mountain where the transfiguration took place (Matthew 17:1-8), and He trusted them to pray with Him in the Garden of Gethsemane. (Matthew 26:36-46) John and Peter were the first male Disciples to be told about the empty tomb. (John 20:2,3) And they got special recognition when Jesus appeared to them as the risen Lord. (John 21:1-7) There is no doubt while Jesus could not grant Salome's request, He did afford James and John the opportunity to become great in His kingdom. James became the first Christian martyr. He was put to death by King Herod Agripa I in A.D. 44. John lived to be an old man and was important in the early church. (Galatians 2:9) He wrote five of the New Covenant books: John, I, II, III John and Revelation. John died in Ephesus at the end of the First Century A.D. (*Pictorial Bible Dictionary*, p. 438.)

This peaceful mother must have been very proud of her sons. They showed great faith and leadership, a force Jesus recognized when he named them *Boanerger* which means *sons of thunder* after they wanted to call down fire from Heaven on an uncooperative Samaritan village. (Luke 9:51-55)

Salome was also granted a special place in the story of Jesus. She was privileged to be among the women who witnessed His crucifixion. (Mark 15:40) And she was one of the first to witness His resurrection. (Mark 16:1)

THE SAMARITAN

John 4:4-43

The Samaritans and the orthodox Jews had a long history of mutual animosity. It began with a chosen people who ultimately chose to disobey their God. In 721 B.C. Assyria invaded Palestine and deported many of the Israelite people and brought in foreign people along with their culture and religions to occupy the province of Samara. (II Kings 17:6-41) In 587 B.C. Babylon also deported people and once again the Israelite people lived in exile. However, King Cyrus (538-529 B.C.) began to allow the Jews to return to their homeland. The return happened from 538 to 458 B.C. when Ezra came to Jerusalem to carry out religious reforms.

Over the years, by marrying the transplanted peoples, the Samaritan Jews became a mixed race. They had also accepted and incorporated foreign religious rites into their religion. Ezra, and later Nehemiah, demanded racial and religious purity. The Samaritans were not allowed to help rebuild the temple. They became hostile and disrupted the lives of the returning Jews. (Nehemiah 2:10-19) An alternate temple was built in Samaria on Mount Gerizim. And although this temple, like the temples in Jerusalem, was destroyed, the Samaritans continued to worship on Mount Gerizim. (John 4:20, 21)

It was no accident that Jesus traveled through this area of Samaria. The New Covenant was being established in all of Palestine. The Samaritans were not overlooked. Jesus came to redeem all people. The woman who came in the heat of the day to Jacob's well near the city of Sychar was able to converse with Jesus about her heritage. Perhaps she had worshipped on the holy mountain. Perhaps she had worshipped many gods. Five different gods were introduced into Samaria. (II Kings 17: 29-34) When Jesus met the woman, He told her about her five husbands. The word translated *husband* can mean *god*. Jeremiah writes, "Behold, the days are coming, says the Lord, when I will make a New Covenant with the house of Israel and the house of Judah, not like the covenant which I made with their fathers when I took them by the hand to bring them out of the land of Egypt, my covenant which they broke, though I was their husband, says the Lord. But this is the covenant which I will make with the house of Israel after those days, says the Lord: I will put my law within them, and I will write it upon their hearts; and I will be their God, and they shall be my people." (Jeremiah 31:31-33)

The wonder of this meeting is not that Jesus spoke with a Samaritan woman, but that He brought the New Covenant to Samaria. Just as the temple in Jerusalem no longer represented the presence of God, neither did Mount Gerizim any longer represent the presence of God. Jesus said, "But the hour is coming, and now is, when the true worshippers will worship the Father in spirit and truth, for such the Father seeks to worship him. God is spirit and those who worship him must worship in spirit and truth. The woman said to him, *I know that Messiah is coming (he who is called Christ); when he comes, he will show us all things.* Jesus said to her, *I who speak to you am he.* (John 4:23-26)

The woman's response to Jesus was typical of all who encounter Jesus: She left her water jar and went to tell others, and "many Samaritans from the city believed in him because of the woman's testimony." (John 4:39a) "And many more believed because of his word. They said to the woman, i*t is no longer because of your words that we believe, for we have heard for ourselves, and we know that this is indeed the Savior of the world.*" (John 4: 41-42) The woman, who encountered Jesus at Jacob's well, found *living water* for herself and was privileged to be the first Christian evangelist in Samaria.

21st Century Perspective

Nothing has changed! Whether we serve in the kitchen or in the pulpit; in our home community or on a mission field in a foreign country, women today, still minister with Jesus.

TO PONDER:

Read Ephesians 3:7 and Ephesians 4:11-16 and think about the following:

- ❖ Name three ministries God has called you to do.

- ❖ What were the results of these ministries?

- ❖ Recall the last ministry you were called to do. How do you expect God to bless this ministry?

- ❖ Have you been called to a task to which you have not yet responded? What is keeping you from accepting the call?

Part One, Chapter Seven, Lesson Twenty-Six

LESSONS
TAUGHT
THROUGH WOMEN

LESSONS TAUGHT THROUGH WOMEN

Jesus taught. Jesus taught about change and the coming of the Kingdom of God. The law would no longer be observed as a burden imposed from the outside that could never be mastered. In the future, the law would be written on the hearts of men and women to be followed as a response to the love of God. Jesus taught through actions and words. He healed on the Sabbath because the Sabbath was given for the benefit of people, not a ritual to be observed. (Luke 6:1-5; 13: 15-16)) He labored and He rested. (Luke 8:23) Jesus prayed and taught His disciples how to pray. (Matthew 6:9-13; Luke 11:1-2) He associated with sinners and had compassion on the sick and dying. He even paid His taxes. (Matthew 17:24-27) Jesus taught the crowds on the hillsides and mountains (Matthew 15:29-30), by the sea (Matthew 4:18), in homes (Luke 10:38), in the synagogues (Luke 4:16), and as he walked along the dusty roads (Luke 24:13f). Jesus taught men, women and children. There were lessons to be learned from Jesus' actions, circumstances and His direct words. It has been said nothing is accomplished or learned until change takes place. Jesus brought about more change in three years than anyone else ever has. Jesus is still changing lives and millions of people have changed lives today because Jesus taught.

THE POOR WIDOW

Luke 21:1f; Mark 12:41-44

A widow had come to the temple to worship. She was found among the general public. Jesus and His Disciples were there. Scribes and Pharisees were there. Undoubtedly the Levites and Priest were serving in the temple.

The offering at the temple was used in thirteen ways. Therefore, there were thirteen different trumpet-shaped receptacles for receiving the offering, so the people could designate their offering for a specific purpose. The Pharisees and Sadducees always made sure their gifts made a lot of noise so people would notice they were giving. The poor widow put in two copper coins which didn't make much noise at all. Jesus pointed out she gave more than all the others because she gave all she had. (Luke 21:4) This was the commitment Jesus was seeking: not an outward show of ritual pomp, but a sincere giving of all.

Earlier Jesus was asked if it was lawful to pay taxes to Caesar. He answered: "render to Caesar the things that are Caesar's and to God the things that are God's." (Luke 20:25) The Denarius has Caesar's picture on it, but people are made in the image of God. (Genesis 1:27) God's picture is reflected in people. So if people give themselves to God; God will not only have the person, but all the person is and all she or he possesses. The poor widow gave all she had. She could not do more.

The lesson teaches God wants our complete devotion and even the poorest woman among us can be the one who gives the most.

THE WOMAN CAUGHT IN ADULTERY

John 8:3-11

Death by stoning was an ancient punishment for adultery still practiced in some countries where cultures are slow to change and religious rites are steeped in Old Covenant usage. In 2002 a Nigerian woman named Safiya was accused of adultery for having a baby with her former husband. Her punishment was to be death by stoning. Nothing is said about punishment for her former husband and the father of her child. Many people came to her aid: "Fifteen heads of state at the Barcelona Summit . . . issued a joint declaration requesting the Nigerian government to save the life of Safiya. As many as 420,000 signatures of protest were handed in to the Nigerian Embassy in Spain and the city of Naples declared Safiya an honorary citizen. In Warsaw, a hundred people demonstrated in front of the Nigerian Embassy." (*Pravda, Ru*, "Stoning to Death in the 21st Century", 3-20-2002, p.1)

The Old Covenant Scriptures do not look favorably on reconciliation of the first relationship after the wife has moved on to be with another man. She is looked on as being damaged or polluted. (Jeremiah 3:1) Adultery in the Old Covenant was always with the wife of another. For example, if a man had sex with his neighbor's wife, he sinned against his neighbor. The man and the woman were subject to death. (Leviticus 20:10) There are warnings, especially in Proverbs, about the evils of wicked women, prostitutes or women who enticed men with their eyes. However, sex with a prostitute was not the same as adultery. Adultery was with another man's wife. The idea was that the offending man was taking something away from another man.

Jesus came not to destroy the law, but to make it full and complete. He said, "You have heard that it was said, *you shall not commit adultery*. But I say to you that every one who looks at a woman lustfully has already committed adultery with her in his heart." (Matthew 5; 27-28)

The first century Jews still lived under Old Covenant law. In John 8:3-11, the Scribes and Pharisees brought a woman to Jesus they said was caught in the act of adultery.

Why did they not take her to the priest? Under the law, the woman would have been subject to the priest. (Numbers 5:11-22) It is clear the Scribes and Pharisees were trying to find fault with Jesus so that they could accuse Him of some wrong doing. Where had they found the woman? And, just how public was her indiscretion? What happened to the man? Why was he not accused? If the woman had been another man's wife, the man should also have been punished. Perhaps she was a prostitute the Pharisees knew. A man that had sex with a prostitute would not have been accused. Sex with a prostitute would hardly count since nothing was taken from a fellow man. Regardless of how this woman came to be caught in adultery, the Scribes and Pharisees used her to test Jesus. (John 8:6) If Jesus said stone the woman, He would appear harsh and unloving. If He said leave her alone, He could be accused of disobeying the Law of Moses. Jesus wrote on the ground and spoke the words we have often heard: "Let him who is without sin among you be the first to throw a stone at her." (John 8:7) Then He wrote on the ground again, giving the men time to examine their own lives. They left—one by one—until Jesus and the woman stood alone. Jesus asked her, *has no one condemned you?* She said *no one, Lord.* (John 8:10-11) This does not mean the woman recognized Jesus as the Messiah. The word used here for *Lord* can also be translated *sir.* However, Jesus did forgive her sin. He challenged her to go and sin no more. One would hope somehow she realized the magnitude of her encounter with Jesus and accepted His pardon and His challenge. "The wages of sin is death." Some are stoned; some receive the death sentence in other ways. "But, the free gift of God is eternal life in Christ Jesus our Lord." (Romans 6:23)

The lesson taught is, "there is no distinction [between male and female] since all have sinned and fall short of the glory of God, [all can receive forgiveness] by His grace as a gift, through the redemption which is in Christ Jesus. . .." (Romans 3:23-24)

WOMAN IN THE CROWD

Luke 11:27-28

". . . a woman in the crowd raised her voice and said to him, *Blessed is the womb that bore you, and the breast that you sucked!* But, he said *Blessed rather are those who hear the word of God and keep it!*"

What do we know about this woman? She was in the crowd. The crowd was following Jesus as He traveled in Galilee possibly near the town of Bethany, near Jerusalem. The Apostles were there; people whom Jesus had healed of physical and mental diseases were there. Perhaps the man who called from the crowd asking Jesus to heal his son was there. (Luke 9:38f) People with demons and some who had been released from their demons were there. Jews were there who accused Jesus of being the devil himself. You could have hardly found a more diverse crowd.

Who was the woman who felt so free as to raise her voice and speak to Jesus? Her opinion reflected that of the first-century Jew. She was the average member of the crowd. Perhaps she was the common person who came out of curiosity to find out about Jesus. She would have believed women were blessed when they had children and cursed when unable to bare children. This motif permeates the Bible from the Old Covenant speaking of Sarah, Rebekah, Rachel and Hannah to the New Covenant and Elizabeth. Jesus came to reorder the attitudes even about motherhood. He said, "blessed rather are those who hear the word of God and keep it" (Luke 11:28) Women are responsible for hearing and keeping God's word--a directive that has implications far beyond the blessings of motherhood.

The lesson taught is devotion to God is the highest priority, surpassing even the priority of motherhood.

MAID IN THE COURTYARD

Mark 14:53-15:1

Jesus had been betrayed by Judas into the hands of an angry mob. After Jesus raised Lazarus from the dead, the chief priest and Pharisees gathered the council and determined "if we let him go on thus, every one will believe in him and the Romans will come and destroy both our holy place and our nation, and Caiaphas the high priest prophesied *that one man should die for the people, and that the whole nation should not perish.*" (John 11:48-50)

A band of soldiers and officers of the Jews took Jesus bound to Annas and Caiaphas, the high priest. Annas and Caiaphas may have lived in homes joined by a courtyard. Peter and John followed the arresting party.

While all four Gospels report Peter denied having known Jesus, each has a slightly different take on the story. John reports a maid of Caiaphas was keeping the door. John knew Caiaphas and therefore gained entrance to the house for himself and Peter. (John 18: 15-16) The maid thought she recognized Peter as being one of Jesus' Disciples. Matthew reports two maids that recognize Peter as a Disciple, one in the courtyard and one on the porch. Or perhaps it was the same maid who approached Peter twice. Luke reports a maid recognized Peter as he stood in the glow of the campfire in the courtyard. Mark reports the same maid spoke to Peter twice. All of the Gospels report the bystanders around the fire said surely Peter was one of the Disciples. John reports a kinsman of the man whose ear Peter cut off when they arrested Jesus recognized Peter as a Disciple. The man who lost his ear was likely a slave of the high priest. (Matthew 26:51) Peter denied Jesus three times before the cock crowed twice as was predicted by Jesus. (Matthew 26:33-34; Mark 14:29-30; Luke 22:33-34)

But who were these maidens? They were most likely young women who worked as domestic servants for Caiaphas, the high priest and were perhaps influenced by the attitude of their employer. According to John, one maid was the keeper of the door. (John 18:16) She seemed to have free rein of the house and courtyard even in the middle of the night. She spoke freely with the participants who had gathered for the mock trial of Jesus. Apparently at least one of the maids had seen Jesus and His disciples before. Maybe she had even listened to Jesus' message. But there is no evidence she understood or believed it. She tried to implicate Peter as an accessory to charges made against Jesus. No doubt, this young woman was an instigator and a trouble-maker. While Jesus was affirming His Messiahship and confirming His destiny, Peter was allowing a maidservant to goad him into denying Jesus. It was the third watch, (Mark 13:35) the cock crowed, and morning came, a new day—a day that would forever change the world.

The lesson taught is one must always be aware of his or her relationship with Jesus because insignificant people and stressful circumstances may cause an otherwise strong person to feel threatened and deny Jesus.

THE WOMAN SINNER

Matthew 26:6f; Mark 14:3-9; Luke 7:36f; John 12:1-8

Several Scriptures give an account of a woman who anoints Jesus with an expensive ointment. (Matthew 26:6f; Mark 14:3-9; Luke 7:36f; John 12:1-8) Each has a slightly different take on who the woman may have been or exactly where Jesus was having dinner when the event occurred.

The story may have gone something like this: When Jesus was in Bethany, He was invited to have dinner with friends. The houses were easily accessed from the street. So when Jesus sat down to eat, a woman from the neighborhood who was a known sinner came in and began to wash His feet with her tears. She dried His feet with her hair, kissed His feet and anointed them with pure nard. The ointment costs approximately 300 denarii, which would have been almost a year's wages. The guests were incensed by her actions; first, because she was a known sinner, and second because it appeared she was wasteful and they felt the money could have been used for the poor. Jesus replied that the host had not provided the service of washing His feet, nor had His host kissed Him. The woman had performed the task of a servant. She may have heard Jesus' message, "I have not come to call the righteous, but sinners to repentance." (Luke 5:32) Jesus forgave her many sins. Her capacity to love matched her capacity for sinning. Jesus said her faith had saved her and she should go in peace. Her actions earned her a place in history and Jesus said she would always be remembered.

The lesson taught is when a person is forgiven much, that person appreciates forgiveness more.

KINGDOM TEACHERS

Jesus taught us to pray "Thy kingdom come, Thy will be done, on earth as it is in heaven." (Matthew 6:10) What does it mean for God's kingdom to come? Jesus used women in His examples to show how the Kingdom of God was developing and how it would be consummated. First, Jesus compares the beginning of the kingdom to a woman giving birth. (John 16:21) There is pain, and anguish involved. (Matthew 11:12) Entering the kingdom is often spoken of as a new birth. Jesus told Nicodemus "Truly, truly, I say to you, unless one is born anew, he cannot see the kingdom of God. Nicodemus said to him, *How can a man be born when he is old? Can he enter a second time into his mother's womb and be born?* Jesus answered, *Truly, truly, I say to you unless one is born of water and the Spirit, he cannot enter the kingdom of God.*" (John 3:3-7)

New beginnings are often violent. This was especially true in the case of Jesus and His disciples. Once the religious establishment realized the birth of a New Covenant was taking place, they constantly sought the demise of Jesus. Secondly, Jesus came not to destroy the Old Covenant, but to make it complete and full of integrity. For example, in the Old Covenant, children were taught to honor their mother and father. The mother received the same honor as the father. (Exodus 20:12) However, Jesus told the Pharisees the old law allowed people to neglect their parents by saying they had given their money, time, etc. to God. (Mark 7:10-12) When a woman has a relative who is a widow, she should not leave that responsibility to the church, but attend to the needs of her family. (I Timothy 5:16)

Under the old law, divorce would be granted to a man for almost any reason. (i.e. hardness of heart) Under the New Covenant, men and women were to leave their parents and become one. Divorce is to be granted only in case of unfaithfulness. "But if the unbelieving partner desires to separate, let it be so; in such case the brother or sister is not bound." (I Corinthians 7: 15) Marriage is used throughout the Bible as a metaphor for entering the kingdom of God. Just as one leaves father and mother to enter into marriage, one must not hold family in a higher position than Jesus when entering and serving in His kingdom. Jesus said those who forsake all to follow Him are His family. (Matthew 19:29)

When Jesus returns, there will be "two women grinding at the mill; one will be taken and one will be left. Watch therefore, for you do not know on what day your Lord is coming. But, know this, that if the householder had known in what part of the night the thief was coming, he would have watched and would not have let his house be broken into. Therefore you also must be ready; for the Son of man is coming at an hour you do not expect." (Matthew 24:41-44) Women must be found faithful and watchful.

The kingdom grows because God searches for the lost person just as the woman in Luke 15:8-10 searched for her lost coin. She lit a lamp, and swept every inch of her house to find the coin which was lost. The kingdom began small, first with John the Baptist, then Jesus, then the Apostles, and Disciples are still being added daily. Jesus demonstrated this principle by telling about the woman who hid leaven in dough. At first the dough was small, but it soon rose to make a large batch. (Matthew 13:33) In these examples we see the image of God working as a female seeking the lost and promoting the growth of God's kingdom.

When the Sadducees tested Jesus about the afterlife (they didn't believe in the resurrection of the dead), they used the example of the levirate marriage. When a man died, his oldest brother married his widow and raised children in his name so that the dead brother wouldn't lose his inheritance. The Sadducees posed the question: if a woman is married and her husband dies, and she marries her husband's brother and this happens seven times, since she has been married to seven different men, whose wife is she in Heaven? Jesus used His answer to teach about Heaven and the resurrection. He told them, "For in the resurrection they neither marry nor are given in marriage, but are like angels in heaven. And as for the resurrection of the dead, have you not read what was said to you by God, *I am the God of Abraham, and the God of Isaac, and the God of Jacob*? He is not God of the dead, but of the living." (Matthew 22:30-33)

"Then the kingdom of heaven shall be compared to ten maidens who took their lamps and went to meet the bridegroom. Five of them were foolish, and five were wise. For when the foolish took their lamps, they took no oil with them; but the wise took flask of oil with their lamps." (Matthew 25:1-4) Women are used as examples of preparedness and must be found ready when Jesus returns for His church. The church is the bride of Christ, and upon His return a great celebration will take place. (Revelation 19:9) The days prior to Jesus' return will be full of turmoil. It will be particularly hard on women who are pregnant or nursing. (Matthew 24:16-21)

The Pharisees wanted to know when the kingdom was coming. Jesus replied, "the kingdom of God is not coming with signs to be observed; nor will they say, *Lo, here it is!* or *There!* for behold the kingdom of God is in the midst of you or within you." (Luke 17:21) Jesus was in the midst of them, and the Holy Spirit now resides within all believers.

The story of the persistent widow and the unjust judge reminds us to continually pray and remain faithful until the end. (Luke 18:2-8) "The Spirit and the Bride say, *Come*." (Revelation 22:17) The kingdom is now and forever!

Some lessons taught through kingdom teachers are: (1) One must be born again to enter the kingdom; (2) Women should care for their elderly relatives; (3) Women should respect and honor their marriages; (4) God is looking to find the lost; (5) The kingdom of God will grow; (6) Everyone should be prepared for Jesus' second coming; (7) Everyone should be persistent in prayer; (8) Prayer and faithfulness are required until Jesus returns.

21st Century Perspective

Whether we realize it or not, the way we live our lives teaches other people. We can learn valuable lessons from observing the lives of the women in the Bible.

TO PONDER:

Read Matthew 5:14-16 and think about the following:

❖ What has God taught through you?

❖ How have you taught others?

❖ In what way are you a light in the world?

❖ Say a prayer that the Light within you will not be hidden but will shine forth to show others the Kingdom of God.

Volume Two, Part Two

GROWING THE CHURCH

Part Two
Concordance

THE BOOK OF ACTS OF THE APOSTLES

Acts is the first written record of *church history* and was probably written by Luke in the third quarter of the first century. Luke is especially aware of the participation of women in the progress and growth of the early church. The Gospel spread from Jerusalem where the Apostles and Disciples were told to wait until they were baptized with the Holy Spirit. (Acts 1: 4-5) "The Apostles, the women, Mary, the mother of Jesus and Jesus' brothers" devoted themselves to prayer as they waited. (Acts 1:14) Acts means *achievements*, *praxis* in Greek, and the achievements of women are highlighted throughout the book of Acts.

The Holy Spirit came on the day of Pentecost fifty days after Easter. It is also the celebration of *First Fruits* for the Jews. The events of Acts 2 turned the holiday into a Christian holiday for the Jesus followers. Three thousand souls received the word and were baptized on the first Pentecost. Peter preached a sermon in which he quoted Joel 2:28f: "and in the last days it shall be, God declares, that I will pour out my Spirit upon all flesh, and your sons and your daughters shall prophesy . . ." (Acts 2:17) There was no doubt in Peter's mind, the *last days* were upon them. The sect who believed Jesus was the Messiah proceeded to live as if Jesus would come back at any moment. They sold their possessions, and "all who believed were together and had all things in common." (Acts 2:44) Ananias and Sapphira were among these individuals. While they sold their land, they were not ready to give all and proceeded to lie about their gift. This story serves to show how women were active participants in the church and Sapphira was held equally responsible with her husband for her actions.

As the church grew it became necessary to have additional people to help care for the widows. Therefore, Stephen and six others were chosen to care for the Greek widows. As a result of being a servant of Jesus, Stephen lost his life. While preaching about Jesus, the Jews "cast him out of the city and stoned him; and the witnesses laid down their garments at the feet of a young man named Saul (Paul)." (Acts 7:58) Saul was later converted to believe in Jesus as the Messiah; however, on this day he was persecuting the Christians: "and on that day a great persecution arose against the church in Jerusalem; and they were scattered throughout the region of Judea and Samaria." (Acts 8:1) Philip, who was also one of the chosen seven, preached in Samaria. "When they believed Philip as he preached the good news about the kingdom of God and the name of Jesus Christ, they were baptized, both men and women." (Acts 8:12)

"Now there was at Joppa a Disciple named Tabitha, which [in Greek] is called Dorcus." (Acts 9:36) Dorcus was raised from the dead that she might continue her good works. Peter traveled as far as Phoenicia, Cyprus and Antioch preaching the word. And, Herod had him arrested. But the *angel of the Lord* rescued him from jail. After Peter came to himself, he went to the house of Mary, mother of John Mark, where people were gathered for a prayer meeting. Again, women were taking an active role in the Jesus movement.

After Paul was converted, he and his company went to Antioch of Pisidia where he preached in the synagogue. And on "the next Sabbath almost the whole city gathered together to hear the word of God." (Acts 13:44) "And the word of the Lord spread throughout the region. But the Jews incited the devout women of high standing and the leading men of the city, and stirred up persecution against Paul and Barnabas, and drove them out of their district." (Acts 13: 50) Women were active, standing their ground on both sides of the Jesus movement.

Barnabus and John Mark went to Cyprus. Paul and Silas went to Syria and Cilicia and "from there to Philippi which was a leading city of the district of Macedonia, and a Roman colony." (Acts 16:12) Paul and Silas found a congregation of women who had come together for prayer. A woman named Lydia became the first Christian in Europe and immediately offered the hospitality of her home to Paul and Silas, where a church was established.

In Thessalonica, Paul and Silas spoke for three weeks at the synagogue: "And some of them were persuaded, and joined Paul and Silas; as did a great many of the devout Greeks and not a few of the leading women." (Acts 17:4) In Beroea "many of them therefore believed, with not a few Greek women of high standing as well as men." (Act 17: 12) Then Paul went to Athens and while at the Areopagus a woman named Damaris accepted Jesus as Lord and Savior. Paul "left Athens and went to Corinth where he found Aquila and Priscilla and stayed with them for a year and a half. From there he sailed for Syria taking Priscilla and Aquila with him. He left them to minister at Ephesus while he went on to Caesarea. After spending some time in Caesarea he departed and went from place to place through the region of Galatia and Phrygia." (Acts 18:22-23)

Continuing to show the relationship and participation of the women in the progress and growth of the early church, Paul "entered the house of Philip the evangelist, who had four unmarried daughters, who prophesied." (Acts 21:8-9) Indeed, the prophecy of Joel had come true.

Luke ends his story with Paul in Rome under house arrest where *he preached unhindered for two whole years.* (Notes, Acts 28: 30-31, RSV.)

FEMALES IN THE BOOK OF ACTS:

Women 1:14; 5:14; 8:3, 12; 16:13; 22:4
Mary the mother of Jesus 1:14
Your daughters 2:17
Maidservants 2:18
Sapphira 5:1
His wife 5:7; 18:2; 24:24
Widows 6:1
Pharaoh's daughter 7:21
Candace 8:27
Queen of the Ethiopians 8:27
Tabitha (a disciple) 9:36, 40
Dorcas (Tabitha) 9:36, 39
Widows 9:39, 41
Mary 12:12
Mother of John 12:12
Maid 12:13
Rhoda (doorkeeper) 12:13
Devout women 13:50
Jewish woman 16:1
Women 16:14; 17:34
Lydia 16:14, 40
Slave girl 16:16
Leading women 17:4
Greek women of high standing 17:12
Damaris 17:34
Priscilla 18:2, 18, 26
The great goddess Artemis 19:27, 28, 34, 35
Our goddess 19:37
Wives 21:5
Four unmarried daughters who prophesied 21:9
Paul's sister 23:16
Drusilla 24:24
Bernice (Queen) 25:13, 23; 26:30

THE BOOK OF ROMANS

In his letter to the Romans, Paul addressed all the saints in Rome. (Romans 1:7) This surely included the women in the church at Rome. In chapter 7:2-6, Paul used the example of a woman who was bound to her husband as long as he lived, but was free to marry another when he died. The concept of marriage is once again used to demonstrate the meaning of the coming of the New Covenant. Paul wrote: "likewise, my brethren, you have died to the law through the body of Christ, so that you may belong to another, to him who has been raised from the dead in order that we may bear fruit of God. While we were living in the flesh, our sinful passions, aroused by the law, were at work in our members to bear fruit for death. But now we are discharged from the law, dead to that we serve not under the old written code but in the new life of the Spirit." (Romans 7:4-6)

The children of promise came through two chosen devoted women, Sarah and Rebekah. (Romans 9: 8-15) God's purpose of election continues: "for He said to Moses, I will have mercy on whom I have mercy, and I will have compassion on whom I have compassion." (Romans 9:15) Paul addressed *everyone among you*. (Romans 12:3) No doubt, there were women among them.

"For as in one body we have many members, and all the members do not have the same function, so we, though many, are one body in Christ, and individually members one of another. Having gifts that differ according to the grace given to us, let us use them: if prophecy, in proportion to our faith; if service, in our serving; he who teaches, in his teaching; he who exhorts, in his exhortation; he who contributes, in liberality; he who gives aid, with

zeal; he who does acts of mercy with cheerfulness." (Romans 12:4-8)

Again, "let every person be subject to the governing authorities." (Romans 13:1) Owe no one anything, except to love one another; for he who loves his neighbor has fulfilled the law! (Romans 13:8) "Let us cast off the works of darkness and put on the armor of light . . . put on the Lord Jesus Christ, and make no provision for the flesh, to gratify its desires." (Romans 14:14) "So each of us shall give account of himself [or herself] to God." (Romans 14:12) In Romans, chapter 16, Paul greets both women and men alike, and 6 of the 24 people he greets are women; women who worked by Paul's side and who were working in the Roman church. These church women served as equals with men, and Paul did not make a distinction in their service.

FEMALES IN THE BOOK OF ROMANS:

Women 1:26, 27
Sarah's womb 4:19
Married women 7:2
Sarah 9:9
Rebecca 9:10
Our sister 16:1
Deaconess of the church
    at Cenchreae 16:1
Prisca 16:3, 12
Mary 16:6

Junias 16:7 May or may
    not have been a
    woman
Tryphosa 16:12
His mother 16:13
Julia 16:15 May or may
    not have been a
    woman
His sister 16:15

THE BOOK OF I CORINTHIANS

"This is one of the most valuable of Paul's letters, not only for the light it throws upon the character and mind of the Apostle and for its vigorous presentation of the Gospel but also for the vivid pictures it brings us of the actual life of a particular local church in the middle of the first century." (I Corinthians, Introduction, RSV.) This section addresses the *actual life* of the women in the Corinthian church.

The church at Corinth had many problems, perhaps the results of having a congregation where the majority of the people came from a community of idolaters. (I Corinthians 6:10-11; 8:7; 12:2) They were following after their leaders instead of Christ. Paul wrote: "what I mean is that each one of you says, *I belong to Paul*, or *I belong to Apollos*, or *I belong to Cephas* or *I belong to Christ*." (I Corinthians 1:12) People were arrogant. Some of the arrogant were women. People were immoral: "A man was living with his father's wife." (I Corinthians 5:1) This sin obviously involved immorality on the part of both a man and a woman. Paul advised, "not to associate with any one who bears the name of brother if he is guilty of immorality or greed, or is an idolater, reviler, drunkard, or robber—not even to eat with such a one." (I Corinthians 5:11) "The body is not meant for immorality, but for the Lord, and the Lord for the body." (I Corinthians 6: 13b)

The Corinthian Church had asked Paul for help with their problems: "now concerning the matters about which the Corinthians had written to Paul" (I Corinthians 7:1):

When men and women are tempted sexually, *"each man should have his own wife and each woman should have her own husband. The husband should give to his wife* her *conjugal rights and likewise the wife to her husband. For the wife does not rule over her own body, but the husband does; likewise the husband does not rule over his own body, but the wife does. Do not refuse one another except perhaps by agreement for a season, that you may devote yourselves to prayer; but then come together again lest Satan tempt you through lack of self-control."* (I Corinthians 7: 2-5)

Paul made a striking statement of equality. "In contemporary Greek Society as well as in Judaism, one of the wife's roles was to be sexually available to her husband. He *owned* rights to her sexuality. But the reverse was not true. The husband had rights to his own sexuality; thus the so-called *double standard.* A man could have sex outside of marriage, or in Judaism, have more than one wife. A woman could not have extramarital affairs, and certainly could not have more than one husband." (*Women of the Bible*, p. 309.) Paul made it clear under the New Covenant women had equal rights and equal responsibilities in matters of marriage and sex.

"To the unmarried and the widows, I [Paul] say that it is well for them to remain single as I do. But if they cannot exercise self-control, they should marry." (I Corinthians 7:8)

"The wife should not separate from her husband (but if she does, let her remain single or else be reconciled to her husband)—and that the husband should not divorce his wife." (I Corinthians 7:10-11)

If either a woman or a man is married to an unbeliever and he or she consents to live with him or her, they should stay married. One may be won to Christ through the other. But if the unbelieving partner wants to separate, let it be so;

in such a case the brother or sister is not bound. (I Corinthians 7:15)

It is better to remain unmarried because "the unmarried woman or girl is anxious about the affairs of the Lord, how to be holy in body and spirit; but the married woman is anxious about worldly affairs, how to please her husband." (I Corinthians 7:34) Paul broke with "rabbinic thought that assumed the significance of women was rooted in their roles as wives and mothers." (*Women of the Bible*, p. 309.)

"Any woman who prays or prophesies with her head unveiled dishonors her head—it is the same as if her head were shaven. For if a woman will not veil herself, then she should cut off her hair; but if it is disgraceful for a woman to be shorn or shaven, let her wear a veil." (I Corinthians 11:5-6) The fact that Paul assumed women will pray and prophesy is important. The question was not one of religion, but one of custom. Women were to show proper respect within the confines of their customs. Paul goes on to say: "Nevertheless, in the Lord, woman is not independent of man and man of woman; for as woman was made from man so man is now born of woman. And, all things are from God." (I Corinthians 11:11-12) Here is found an explicit defense of the equality of woman and man in the New Covenant. Paul overturned the traditional argument of the priority of the male in the creation narrative.

People were not observing the Lord's Supper properly. Instead they were eating greedily and getting drunk.

The Corinthians needed instructions about spiritual gifts and the importance of all parts of the body of Christ. Paul spoke to all the church when he said, "and God has appointed in the Church first Apostles, second prophets, third teachers, then workers of miracles, then healers, helpers, administrators, speakers in various kinds of tongues. Are all Apostles? Are all prophets? Are all teachers? Do all work miracles? Do all possess gifts of healing? Do all speak with tongues? Do all interpret? But earnestly desire the higher gifts." (I Corinthians 12:28-31)

Paul tells them to love. "Make love your aim, and earnestly desire the spiritual gifts, especially that you may prophesy." (I Corinthians 14:1)

Next, there is the paragraph which has caused so much discussion: "As in all the churches of the saints, the women should keep silence in the churches. For they are not permitted to speak, but should be subordinate, as even the law says. If there is anything they desire to know, let them ask their husbands at home." (I Corinthians 14:33b-35a.) Some theologians believe these words did not come from Paul. "The strength and clarity of I Corinthians 11:11-12 means that the directive that women must keep silent in church cannot come from the pen of Paul. It is believed to have been added later to be brought into line with the non-Pauline I Timothy 2:11-14." (*Paul, A Critical Life*, p. 290.) Perhaps the women of Corinth were behaving badly and needed to keep silent. Timothy was in Ephesus when he received the first letter. (I Timothy; *Women of the Bible*, p. 319.) Perhaps, the words in I Timothy 2:11-12: "Let a woman learn in silence with all submissiveness. I permit no woman to teach or to have authority over men; she is to keep silent," were directed to Timothy because he was scheduled to go to Corinth to help with the problem. (I Corinthians 16:10) Paul certainly did not mean for all women to keep silent just as he did not mean for all men to keep silent when he wrote to Titus: "for there are many insubordinate men, empty talkers and deceivers, especially the circumcision party; they must be silenced, since they are upsetting whole families by teaching for base gain what they have no right to teach." (Titus 1:10-11)

FEMALES IN THE BOOK OF I CORINTHIANS:

Chloe's people 1:11
Father's wife 5:1
Prostitute 6:15, 16
Woman 7:1, 13; 11:3, 5
His own wife 7:2
Woman her own husband 7:2
His wife 7:3, 14, 33
Her conjugal rights 7:3
Wife 7:3, 4, 10-12, 16, 27, 39; 9:5

Widows 7:8
Unbelieving wife 7:14
Unmarried (Greek virgins) 7:25
Girl (Greek virgin) 7:28
Unmarried woman or girl 7:34
Married woman 7:34
Married woman 7:34
Woman 14:34
Prisca 16:1

THE BOOK OF II CORINTHIANS

II Corinthians does not address men and women separately.

FEMALES IN THE BOOK OF II CORINTHIANS:

Daughters 6:18
Bride 11:2

Eve 11:3

THE BOOK OF GALATIONS

Galations addresses women only indirectly in 6:10 when Paul tells the Galations "let us do good to all men, and especially those who are of the household of faith."

FEMALES IN THE BOOK OF GALATIANS:

Female 3:28
Free woman 4:22-23, 30-31

Hagar 4:24-25
Our mother 4:26

THE BOOK OF EPHESIANS

Ephesians is addressed to *the saints who are also faithful in Christ Jesus*. (Ephesians 1:1) They are told, "be subject to one another out of reverence for Christ. Wives, be subject to your husbands, as to the Lord. For the husband is the head of the wife as Christ is head of the church, his body, and is Himself its Savior. As the church is subject to Christ, so let wives also be subject in everything to their husbands. Husbands, love your wives, as Christ loved the church and gave himself up for her, . . ." (Ephesians 5:23-25) A good marriage is a prototype of Christ and the Church.

FEMALES IN THE BOOK OF EPHESIANS:

Wives 5:22, 24-25, 28
Wife 5:23

His wife 5:28, 33
Mother 5:31; 6:1

THE BOOK OF PHILIPPIANS

Philippians is addressed to *all the saints in Christ Jesus who are in Philippi with the bishops and deacons.* (Philippians 1:1) Paul encouraged *Euodia and Syntyche to agree in the Lord.* "And, I ask you also, true yokefellows, help these women, for they have labored side by side with me in the gospel." Women were actively engaged with Paul in the church and Paul certainly approved of their work.

FEMALES IN THE BOOK OF PHILIPPIANS:

Euodia 4:2   Women 4:3
Synthche 4:2

THE BOOK OF COLOSSIANS

In Colossians 3:12-14, Paul tells us how the Colossians and we should act as Christians:

"Put on then, as God's chosen ones, holy and beloved, compassion, kindness, lowliness, meekness, and patience, forbearing one another and, if one has a complaint against another, forgiving each other; as the Lord has forgiven you, so you also must forgive. And above all these put on love, which binds everything together in perfect harmony."

Then Paul writes; wives should be subject to their husbands and husbands should love their wives. The *house tables* in the Old Covenant never required anything of the husband. In the New Covenant marital relationships were made reciprocal. Paul again shows his concern and support for women by greeting Nympha and the church that met in her home. (Colossians 4:15, RSV.)

FEMALES IN THE BOOK OF COLOSSIANS:

Wives 3:18, 19	Nympha 4:15

THE BOOK OF I THESSALONIANS

I Thessalonians is addressed to a church who was immature, deprived of their leader, and persecuted by the Jewish leaders of the Synagogue. (I Thessalonians, Introduction, RSV.)

FEMALES IN THE BOOK OF I THESSALONIANS:

Wives 4:4   Woman with child 5:3

THE BOOK OF II THESSALONIANS

II Thessalonians was written about a year after the first letter to the Thessalonian Church, and again Paul addressed the whole church. Nothing specific is addressed to women.

FEMALES IN THE BOOK OF II THESSALONIANS:

None

GROWING THE CHURCH

THE BOOK OF I TIMOTHY

"The two letters to Timothy and the one to Titus, commonly called the *Pastorals*, are similar in character and in the problems they raise concerning authorship. It is difficult to ascribe them in their present form to the Apostle Paul." (I Timothy, Introduction, RSV.) Chapter 2:8-12 gives instructions for men and women: "I desire then that in every place the men should pray, lifting holy hands without anger or quarreling; also that women should adorn themselves modestly and sensibly in seemly apparel, not with braided hair or gold or pearls or costly attire but by good deeds, as befits women who profess religion. Let a woman learn in silence with all submissiveness. I permit no woman to teach or to have authority over men; she is to keep silent." And in 3:8-13, instructions are given for deacons:

"Deacons likewise must be serious, not double-tongued, not addicted to much wine, not greedy for gain; they must hold the mystery of the faith with a clear conscience. And let them also be tested first; then if they prove themselves blameless let them serve as deacons. The women likewise must be serious, no slanderers, but temperate, faithful in all things. Let deacons be the husband of one wife, and let them manage their children and their households well; for those who serve well as deacons gain a good standing for themselves and also great confidence in the faith which is in Christ Jesus."

Chapter 5 addresses how Christians should treat each other: As concerning women—"treat older women like mothers, younger women like sisters, in all purity. Honor widows who are *real widows* (those left without support) . . . Let a widow be enrolled if she is not less than sixty years of age, having been the wife of one husband; and she must be well attested for her good deeds, as one who has brought up children, shown hospitality, washed the feet of the saints, relieved the afflicted, and devoted herself to doing good in every way. . . . So I would have younger widows marry, bear children, rule their households, and give the enemy no occasion to revile us. . . . If a believing woman has relatives who are widows, let her assist them; let the church not be burdened, so that it may assist those who are real widows." (I Timothy 5:1-16.)

FEMALES IN THE BOOK OF I TIMOTHY:

Mothers 1:9; 5:2
Women 2:9-11; 3:11
Woman 2:12, 14-15
Eve 2:13
Wife 3:2, 12; 5:9
Older women 5:2

Younger women 5:2
Widows 5:3, 15
Real widows 5:3-5, 15
Younger widows 5:11, 14
Believing women 5:15

THE BOOK OF II TIMOTHY

The books of I and II Timothy are addressed to Timothy. "The second letter to Timothy is an earnest pastoral from a veteran missionary to a younger colleague, urging endurance as the main quality of a preacher of the gospel." (II Timothy, Introduction, RSV.) The veteran missionary teaches Timothy about the last days when "weak women will be burdened with sin and swayed by various impulses, who will listen to anybody and . . . never arrive at a knowledge of the truth." (II Timothy 3:6-7) Women are again included in the greetings. Prisca and Claudia are mentioned.

FEMALES IN THE BOOK OF II TIMOTHY:

Your grandmother 1:5
Lois 1:5
Your mother 1:5
Eunice 1:5

Weak women 3:6
Prisca 4:19
Claudia 4:21

THE BOOK OF TITUS

This letter is addressed directly to Titus, a man born of Greek parents who was twice sent on urgent missions to Corinth. (Titus, Introduction, RSV.) Paul tells us to "teach what benefits sound doctrine. Bid the older men be temperate, serious, sensible, sound in faith, in love, and in steadfastness. Bid the older women likewise to be reverent in behavior, not to be slanderers or slaves to drink; they are to teach what is good, and to train the young women to love their husbands and children, to be sensible, chaste, domestic, kind, and submissive to their husbands, that the word of God may not be discredited." (Titus 2:2-5)

FEMALES IN THE BOOK OF TITUS:

Wife 1:6   Younger women 2:4
Older women 2:3

THE BOOK OF PHILEMON

Philemon is another personal letter which is addressed to Philemon and his wife Apphia. Paul asked them to receive their *run-away* slave, Onesimus, who had become a Christian, back into their home as a brother in Christ.

FEMALES IN THE BOOK OF PHILEMON:

Apphia 1:2   Sister 1:2

In summary, Paul included women in ministry, acknowledged them as partners in spreading the gospel and supported them as leaders in the local churches. He also promoted equal rights for women in familial relationships. God gives spiritual gifts to all of his church members. Women of the early church were given gifts which were used to grow the church and further the Gospel: "what Paul intended to communicate was simply that Christianity, far from requiring radical or revolutionary changes in the social order, offered every person the opportunity to find spiritual fulfillment—whatever that person's station in life." (*Women of the Bible*, p. 312.)

THE BOOK OF HEBREWS

It is reasonable to surmise when there are no specific instructions regarding women or men the Scripture is equally beneficial to both genders. "The recipients of this letter (we do not know who they were) were on the point of giving up their Christian faith and returning to the Jewish beliefs and practices of their ancestors." (Hebrews, Introduction, RSV.) The unknown writer lays out an argument in Hebrews still valid for Christians today of how Jesus is superior to all that existed in the Old Covenant. Therefore, it is likely the congregation to which the Book of Hebrews was addressed was mostly Jewish. Some believe Paul wrote this letter, but others suggest "Priscilla was the author of Hebrews, but that suggestion is not supported by proof." (*All the Women of the Bible*, p. 229.) "Some early church leaders attributed the authorship of the Epistle to the Hebrews to Barnabus." (*Pictorial Bible Dictionary*, p. 98.) Whoever the author, the person likely knew Paul well. Faith knows no gender and this treatise is packed with encouragement for the male or female who is struggling with his or her faith. The following is a list of the main points made in the Book of Hebrews:

(1) Jesus is superior to the prophets.

(2) Jesus is superior to angels.

(3) Jesus is superior to Moses.

(4) Jesus' sacrifice is superior to animal sacrifices.

(5) Jesus is a superior High Priest.

(6) Jesus has a superior ministry.

(7) Jesus is the superior mediator of the New Covenant.

"Now faith is the assurance of things hoped for, the conviction of things not seen. For by it the *men of old* received divine approval." (Hebrews 11:1-2) A roll call of heroes and heroines of faith reinforces this exhortation. Sarah and Rahab are listed alongside Abel, Enoch, Noah, Abraham, Isaac, Jacob, Esau, Moses, Gideon, Barak, Samson, Jephthah, David, Samuel and the prophets. "Jesus is able for all time to save those who draw near to God through Him, since he always lives to make intercession for them." (Hebrews 7:25) The writer of Hebrews tells the church not to *neglect to show hospitality to strangers*, (Hebrews 13:20) *let marriage be held in honor among all, and let the marriage bed be undefiled*, (Hebrews 13:4) *be free from the love of money, be content with what you have*, (Hebrews 13:5) *and obey your leaders and submit to them.* (Hebrews 13:17)

FEMALES IN THE BOOK OF HEBREWS:

Sarah 11:11
Son of Pharaoh's
 daughter 11:24

Rahab 11:31
Women 11:35

THE BOOK OF JAMES

James, the brother of Jesus (Matthew 13:55) is believed to have been the leader of the early Jerusalem Church (Galatians 1:18-19) and is likely the author of the Book of James. After Peter was miraculously released from prison, he went to the house of Mary, mother of John Mark, where a prayer meeting was taking place. Peter instructed the gathering to *tell this to James and to the brethren*, (Acts 12:17b) indicating James was a person of importance in the early church.

The book of James is addressed to the *twelve tribes in the dispersion*, being symbolic of the Christian Jews who were scattered after the stoning of Stephen: "and on that day a great persecution arose against the church in Jerusalem; and they were all scattered throughout the region of Judea and Samaria, except the Apostles." (Acts 8:1) "It would not be surprising if they thought of themselves as the *twelve tribes—the true Israel*." (*Pictorial Bible Dictionary*, p. 402) The book of James is very Jewish and was probably written in the early 60's A.D. before many Gentiles became a part of the Christian movement.

The women may have been somewhat limited, adhering to Jewish customs. The book of James ignores women with the exception of instructions to *visit widows*. However, the actions of Abraham and Rahab are used to show how *faith by itself, if it has no works is dead*. (James 2:17) "And in the same way was not also Rahab the harlot justified by works when she received the messengers and sent them out another way? For as the body apart from the spirit is dead, so faith apart from works is dead." (James 2:25-26) "Abraham and Rehaab represent two extremes: the friend of God and the harlot; but both were justified by God." (Notes: James 2:25, RSV.)

This practical letter on how to give faith substance by putting it into action is beneficial to women as well as men. The customs in which women found themselves in the early church, or in which women find themselves today put no limitations on faith. Where there is faith, works will follow.

FEMALES IN THE BOOK OF JAMES:

Widows 1:27   Rahab 2:25
Sister 2:15

THE BOOK OF I PETER

"Tradition uniformly asserts that Peter went to Rome, that he labored there, and there in his old age suffered martyrdom under Nero. The embellished tradition that he was bishop of Rome for 25 years is contrary to all New Testament evidence." (*Pictorial Bible Dictionary*, p. 642) The New Covenant evidence established Peter's close relationship with Jesus, (Matthew 16:13-18 and 17:1-5) and paints a picture of his erratic behavior and personality. (Matthew 26:33-35, 69-75) Although Peter preached forcibly on many occasions including the day of Pentecost, (Acts 2:14-36) there is no information about him in the Bible, establishing or leading a church with the exception of the Jerusalem church where Peter was apparently in charge when Ananias and Sapphira lied about their offering. (Acts 5:1-10) It appears they were still meeting in the Temple at that time. This does, however, give some insight into how Peter treated women in the early church. He obviously made no distinction between women and men. Sapphira was allowed to approach the altar and give account for herself, and in the end she received the same punishment as her husband. (Acts 5:1-12)

On the day of Pentecost there were people from Mesopotamia, Judea, Cappadocia, Pontus and Asia who heard Peter's message in their own language. (Acts 2:6-9) The book of I Peter is addressed to the exiles in Dispersion who were being persecuted. Women were most certainly among them. "It is almost certain that many of these Cappadocian Jews were converted on the day of Pentecost." (*Pictorial Bible Dictionary*, p. 147.) The Romans had built roads that made Cappadocia accessible to travelers. Peter also addressed the exiles in Pontus, the homeland of Aquila; Galatia to whom Paul had written, the ancient city of Bithynia and Asia, all of which were in the northern part of Asia Minor where women were allowed privileges often denied in other areas.

Peter appeared to have a high regard for women. He traveled with his wife, (I Corinthians 9:5) raised Dorcus from the dead, (Acts 9:36-43) and was with Jesus when he raised Jarius's daughter from the dead. (Luke 8:4-56; Matthew 9:18-26; Mark 5:21-43) Peter gives the following instructions to women:

"Likewise you wives, be submissive to your husbands, so that some, though they do not obey the word, may be won without a word by the behavior of their wives, when they see your reverent and chaste behavior. Let not yours be the outward adorning with braiding of hair, decoration of gold, and wearing of fine clothing, but let it be the hidden person of the heart with the imperishable jewel of a gentle and quiet spirit, which in God's sight is very precious. So once the holy women who hoped in God used to adorn themselves and were submissive to their husbands, as Sarah obeyed Abraham, calling him Lord. And you are now her children if you do right and let nothing terrify you." (I Peter 3:1-6)

Then Peter, as does Paul, addresses men and how they should behave toward their wives. This is the beauty of Christianity. There is no difference between the male and the female. Both have responsibilities in their relationships that will honor God and grow the kingdom.

Christian men and women were experiencing the madness of Nero during this time of persecution (around A.D. 64) and needed encouragement and instruction on how to stay the course. The book of I Peter ends with a greeting: "she who is at Babylon, [symbolic Rome] who is likewise chosen, sends you greetings." (I Peter 5:13) Who is this chosen female? Perhaps she is Peter's wife or another individual or the church at Rome. There is little word on the subject and questions remain.

FEMALES IN THE BOOK OF I PETER:

Wives 3:1	Woman 3:7
Holy women 3:5	She who is at Babylon
Sarah 3:6	5:13
Your wives 3:7	

THE BOOK OF II PETER

Second Peter is highly contested and was the last book of the Bible to be accepted into the Canon. "The tradition that this letter is the work of the Apostle Peter was questioned in early times, and internal indications are almost decisive against it." (II Peter, Introduction, RSV.) It is likely the book was written in the second century by someone wanting to bring honor to Peter. The author does not address women specifically but addresses "those who have obtained a faith of equal standing with ours in the righteousness of our God and Savior Jesus Christ." (II Peter 1:1) He tells them:

"make every effort to supplement your faith with virtue, and virtue with knowledge, and knowledge with self-control, and self-control with steadfastness, and steadfastness with godliness, and godliness with brotherly affection, and brotherly affection with love. For if these things are yours and abound, they keep you from being ineffective or unfruitful in the knowledge of our Lord Jesus Christ." (II Peter 1:5-8)

Women were among the faithful who received these words, and women have continued to be faithful throughout history.

FEMALES IN THE BOOK OF II PETER:

None

THE BOOK OF JUDE

Tradition affirms Jude was written by the brother of James and Jesus in order to warn the church against false teachers. He reminded them about what happened to the fallen angels and the people of Sodom and Gomorrah, (Jude 1:6-7) and encouraged them to rely on "him who is able to keep you from falling and to present you without blemish before the presence of his glory with rejoicing, to the only God, our Savior through Jesus Christ our Lord. . ." (Jude 1:24-25)

FEMALES IN THE BOOK OF JUDE:

None

THE BOOK OF JOHN

(The man who wrote it and the women who helped shape it)

John was Jesus' first cousin. His mother was Salome who was thought to be Mary's sister. His father was Zebedee. They belonged to the employer class, evidenced by a fishing business and hired servants. In much the same way as James, John reflected his Jewish roots in his writings and most likely followed John the Baptist before embracing the Jesus movement. He was personally involved in Jesus' ministry and was part of the *inner circle.* (Peter, James, John) The *inner circle* was present at the transfiguration, (Matthew 17:1; Mark 9:2; Luke 9:28) and at numerous places where Jesus raised people from the dead. (Luke 8:40-56; Matthew 9:18-26; Mark 5:21-43) "John was with Jesus during His seven-month sojourn in the country of Judea, calling the people to repentance and baptism." (*Pictorial Bible Dictionary,* p. 437; John 4:2) Jesus had climbed to Judea's highest point in the noon-day sun when He came to Jacob's well where he sought water for Himself. Here He took the opportunity to teach a woman about *living water.* The Disciples who were traveling with Jesus went into the city to buy food. (John 4:8) Jesus told the woman at the well about her life and she believed He was the Messiah. When the Disciples returned and saw Jesus, "they marveled that He was talking with a woman." (John 4:27) This no doubt reflects John's attitude toward women and especially toward Samaritan women. Jews looked on all Samaritans with contempt because they were *half-breeds.* However, John does give the woman credit for taking the Gospel to many of the people in her city. (John 4:39)

Jesus loved John and at the cross as Jesus was dying, He gave John the responsibility of caring for His mother.

Tradition has it, John did care for Jesus' mother and they lived out their older years in Ephesus. However, some think John remained in Jerusalem until Mary died and eventually went to Ephesus where he apparently died. (*Biblical Illustrator*, Winter, 1997-98, p 14.)

Paul mentions that Peter and John were pillars of the church in Jerusalem and that they gave him the right hand of fellowship. (Galatians 2:9) However, there is very little evidence of how John worked with women. John wrote the Books of John, Revelation, I, II and III John. "He was exiled on the Island of Patmos in 95 A.D. by the Emperor Domitian where he received a vision and wrote the Book of Revelation." (*Pictorial Bible Dictionary*, p 626., Notes, Revelation 1:9-20, RSV.)

The Gospel of John repeatedly shows women in a negative light. The woman at the well was a Samaritan and an adulteress. (4:7-30) John certainly would not have talked with the woman and marveled that Jesus did. John reports Jesus' first miracle of turning water into wine at the marriage of Cana where Mary comes across as a rather pushy Jewish mother. However, Jesus is seen spending time with her. (John 2:12)

In John 8:3f, as in the other Gospels, a woman caught in adultery is brought to Jesus, but nothing is reported about the man with whom the sin was committed. John appears to include Martha and Mary only because they're significant to the death and resurrection of Lazarus and the magnificence of Jesus' passion toward the cross. John portrays them as cooks and servants. (11:5) John tells of Martha's confession of faith (11:27) and of Jesus' compassion for Mary when He wept. (11:35) Mary is portrayed as understanding Jesus' mission because she *anointed Him for His burial.* (12:7)

In the Book of John, the maid in the courtyard confronted Peter only once. Peter is confronted by the people as they warmed themselves around the fire and also by a kinsman of the servant whose ear he cut off. John reported three women with the name, Mary, standing by the cross so he could report how Jesus asked him to care for His mother. However, he does give Mary Magdalene credit for getting to the tomb first, but John gives himself credit for outrunning Peter making him the first male Disciple to arrive at the tomb.

FEMALES IN THE BOOK OF JOHN:

Mother of Jesus 2:1, 3
Woman 2:4; 4:9-10, 11, 15, 16, 19, 21, 25, 27-28, 41; 8: 3-4; 16:21; 19:26; 20:13, 15
His mother 2:5, 12; 19:25-26
Mother's womb 3:4
Bride 3:29
Woman of Samaria 4:7, 9
Samaritan woman 4:9
Woman's testimony 4:39
Village of Mary 11:1
Her sister Martha 11:1
Sister 11:1

Martha 11:1, 5, 19-21, 24, 30, 39; 12:2
Mary 11:2, 19-20, 28, 31-32, 45; 12:3; 20:11, 16
Sisters 11:3
Her sister 11:5, 28
Daughter of Zion 12:15
Maid 18:17
His mother's sister 19:25
Mary, wife of Clopas 19:25
Mary Magdalene 19:25; 20:1, 18
Your mother 19:27

THE BOOK OF I JOHN

John addressed the book of First John to *my little children* and tells them not to love in word or speech, but in deed and truth. (I John 3:17) He wrote specifically to fathers and young men, but has nothing to say to mothers and young women.

FEMALES IN THE BOOK OF I JOHN:

None

THE BOOK OF II JOHN

The book of Second John is addressed to a specific church.

FEMALES IN THE BOOK OF II JOHN:

Elect Lady (the church) 1:1	Elect sister (another church) 1:13

THE BOOK OF III JOHN

The book of Third John is addressed to a specific person named Gaius.

FEMALES IN THE BOOK OF III JOHN:

None

THE BOOK OF REVELATION

Revelation contains instructions for the first-century Christians who were suffering persecution. Revelation also contains veiled messages about the second coming of Jesus, and the end of the age judgments. There is little about women in Revelation, with the exception of some female imagery about the church. The book of Revelation gives encouragement to all Christians who are waiting and hoping for Jesus' return.

FEMALES IN THE BOOK OF REVELATION:

The woman Jezebel 2:20
Prophetess 2:20
Woman's hair 9:8
Woman clothed with the sun 12:1
Woman 12:4-6, 13-17; 17:4-9, 18
Great harlot 17:1

Woman sitting on a scarlet beast 17:3
Harlot 17:16
Queen 18:7
Widow 18:7
Bride 18:23; 19:7; 21:2, 9; 22:17
Wife (of the Lamb) 21:9

Part Two, Chapter One, Lesson Twenty-Seven

THE CHURCH

THE FIRST CENTURY CHURCH

The foundations for the church were laid in the precepts and functions of the assembly that first met in the tabernacle in the wilderness. At first God met Moses on the Holy Mountain and then with the people in the tabernacle. In time, the presence of God was moved to Solomon's temple. When God became incarnate in Jesus Christ and dwelled among humans on the Earth, a transformation took place. A New Covenant emerged which would fulfill the predictions of Isaiah 53:12 and Daniel 7:14. After Jesus was raised from the dead, the Holy Spirit came to dwell in the hearts of individuals who make Jesus Lord of their lives.

When Peter made his confession; *You are the Christ, the Son of the living God*, Jesus answered, "Blessed are you Simon Bar-Jona, for flesh and blood has not revealed this to you, but my Father who is in Heaven. And I tell you, you are Peter, and on this rock I will build my church . . .." (Matthew 16:15-18)

And, the church began to take form. The earliest creed or confessional of the church was *Jesus is Lord*. At first the Gospel message was preached to the Jews. Jesus and His Disciples went to the synagogue on the Sabbath; and for many years after Jesus' resurrection, Jesus' followers remained a *sect* within Judaism. Apparently the early Christians had no intention of separating themselves from Judaism. The Jewish religion was not of one mind and tolerated internal sects with different beliefs. For example, the Sadducees did not believe in the resurrection of the dead. (Acts 23:8) There were the Scribes and Pharisees, who insisted on extreme adherence to the Law. It was said they would strain at a gnat and swallow a camel. (Matthew 23:24) The Zealots were the patriotic militant party. (*Pictorial Bible Dictionary*, p. 908; Luke 6:15 and Acts

1:13) The Essenes lived a closed and separate life: "they were ascetics and observed the Law scrupulously; but in worship they faced the sun rather than the temple in Jerusalem, for which they felt contempt." (*Oxford Dictionary of the Bible*, p. 121.) The Nazarites took vows and declared moratoriums on cutting the hair and drinking strong drinks. (e.g. John The Baptist) The Jews were even more diverse when you take into account the orthodox Jew, the proselyte Jew, and the God-fearers who worshipped at the synagogue. Women and non-Jews were in positions of lesser authority.

While there is evidence both Sadducees and Pharisees were threatened by the Jesus movement, it was not until A.D. 85 that the threat to the establishment was sufficient enough to cause an anti-Christian benediction to be published. It appeared this new way of thinking could no longer be tolerated. However, "the Christians were not totally distinct from Jewry until after the Bar-Cochba Revolt in A.D. 135." (*Evangelism in the Early Church*, p. 78.)

Affiliation with Judaism afforded the church some protection in the first century seeing Jews were protected under Roman law. Some Jews who rejected Jesus were looking for a military Messiah. They failed to see how the Messiah could be one crucified on a cross, (Galatians 3:12-13) seeing the weakness of the cross and failing to see the power of the cross in the resurrection. On the other hand, many Jews did believe; in fact, the first converts and Disciples were Jews.

The first century Christians not only worshipped at the synagogue, but established churches in their homes. (Colossians 4:15; Philemon 1:2; Romans 16:5; I Corinthians 16:19) Though there were many *house churches*, Paul spoke of them collectively as *the church*. (I

Corinthians 12:28; 14:12; 15:9; 16:19) Jesus has promised where two or more are gathered in His name, He will be there. (Matthew 18:20)

No other time in history had been so ready and right for the coming of the Messiah. The known world was at relative peace under Roman rule. The prophets of old such as Isaiah who had prophesied about the coming Messiah (Isaiah 35:5 and Isaiah 61:1f) had died, and there was a void and a hunger for a word from God. Also, in the Greek world, the philosophers had debated the merits of one God who was all powerful to replace the pantheon. In general, many people were searching for a better way. Paul, in witnessing to the Greeks, used their idea to persuade some to believe in Jesus. (Acts 17:22f)

"Some also of the Epicurean and Stoic philosophers met Paul. And some said, *what would this babbler say? Others said, he seems to be a preacher of foreign divinities*—because he preached Jesus and the resurrection. And they took hold of him and brought him to the Are-op'agus, saying, *May we know what this new teaching is which you present?* . . . So Paul, standing in the middle of the Are-op'agus, said: *Men of Athens, I perceive that in every way you are very religious. For as I passed along, and observed the objects of your worship, I found also an altar with this inscription, 'To an unknown god.' What therefore you worship as unknown, this I proclaim to you* . . . Now when they heard of the resurrection of the dead, some mocked; but others said, *We will hear you again about this.*' So Paul went out from among them. But some men joined him and believed, among them Dionys'ius the Are-op'agite and a woman named Dam'aris and others with them." (Acts 17:18-19; 22-23; 32-34) Men and women were being added to the church. (Acts 5:14) This new personalized religion appealed to the Greeks for many reasons. There were no class restrictions; women, slaves and poor people could find a place of honor and service. A non-Jew did not have to take second place in order to join. There were no food restrictions and circumcision was not required.

The Roman government required business people to participate in a trade guild. The guilds often met where individuals came into contact with Greek gods. Christians refused to pay attention to the gods and refused to repeat the message *Caesar is Lord*. Christians could not say *Caesar is Lord* and also profess *Jesus is Lord*. Therefore, many Christians lost their jobs and their business contacts: "The attempt of certain groups to work out a form of compromise so essential to the social comfort, and indeed livelihood of many Christians led to the strong reproaches of Jude, II Peter and Revelation 2 and 3." (*Pictorial Bible Dictionary*, p. 866.)

Even so many people were converting to Christianity. In fact, the silversmiths who produced statues of idol gods were worried they were going to lose their livelihoods: "About that time there arose no little stir concerning the Way. For a man named Deme'trius, a silversmith, who made silver shrines of Ar'temis, brought no little business to the craftsmen. There he gathered together, with the workmen of like occupation, and said, *Men, you know that from this business we have our wealth. And you see and hear that not only at Ephesus but almost throughout all Asia this Paul has persuaded and turned away a considerable company of people, saying that gods made with hands are not gods. And there is danger not only that this trade of ours may come into disrepute but also that the temple of the great goddess Ar'temis may count for nothing, and that she may even be deposed from her magnificence, she whom all Asia and the world worship.*" (Acts 19:23-27)

THE COVENANT WOMAN

Rome turned on the Christians. The Jesus movement was not only changing lives, but society was changing. Money and the economy became the issue. The Greeks accused Christians of being atheist because they had no image for their worship. Because Christians met in secret, observed the *Lord's Supper* or *Eucharist* and spoke of loving their brothers and sisters, some Greeks accused them of incest and cannibalism. While many Greeks fed on these rumors, "the well-informed knew quite well that they were false: thus Pliny could discover nothing depraved in the deaconesses he found taking part in the Christian assemblies, and declared himself impressed that the Christians *bound themselves by an oath (sacramento) not to commit any crime, be it adultery, robbery or bribage.* He records when they met for a meal—the Agape, no doubt—the food they consumed was *of an ordinary kind and quite innocent.*" (*Evangelism in the Early Church*, p. 39.)

But, the people in the early church were not perfect. The Corinthian church had problems: immorality, boasting, greed, idolatry, revilers, drunkards, robbers, adulterers, sexual perverts, divisions among Christians, impurity and licentiousness. Paul gave instructions to women and to men about their conduct. At one point the Corinthian women were told to keep silent. (I Corinthians 14:34) However, there was also a time when insubordinate men were told to be silent. (Titus 2:1-8)

The language of the New Covenant is inclusive and without a doubt when one reads: little children, Christians, saints, the twelve tribes or exiles in dispersion (those who fled persecution), the church or beloved, it includes woman and man, slave and free, Jew and Greek, and anyone who makes Jesus Lord of his or her life. Peter addressed his letters to new converts of which many were women.

In C. H. Dodd's *The Apostolic Preaching and its Development*, we find six points the early church used in her mission to the world: " (1) The age of fulfillment has dawned; (2) This has taken place through the ministry, death and resurrection of Jesus; (3) By virtue of the resurrection, Jesus has been exalted to the right hand of God, as Messianic head of the new Israel; (4) The Holy Spirit in the Church is the sign of Christ's present power and glory; (5) The Messianic Age will shortly reach its consummation in the return of Christ,; (6) And finally, the kerygma always closes with an appeal for repentance, the offer of forgiveness and the Holy Spirit, and the promise of salvation, that is the life of the Age to come to those who enter the community." (Ibid., p. 60.) The early church had her belief in the risen Lord and the Holy Spirit to guide her. And through the efforts of Paul, Luke, Peter, James, John, Matthew, Mark and other Disciples, the church has received instructions for living through faith. There were and are obstacles to overcome, but the law remains the same: *"You shall love the Lord your God with all your heart, and with all your soul, and with all your mind.* This is the great and first commandment. And a second is like it, *you shall love your neighbor as yourself.* On these two commandments depend all the law and the prophets." (Matthew 22:36-40)

After Paul's death, women's leadership roles in the church declined. The belief in the immediate return of Jesus was less intense; the Christian church broke away from Judaism, the church began more and more to reflect society, and women lost some of their status. However, as it was under the Old Covenant, and as it has been throughout history, when women walk with Jesus and are called by God, they rise above the culture and break through barriers to answer His call in order to carry out His purpose for their lives and for the world.

APOSTLES AND DISCIPLES

It can fairly be said that all Apostles are Disciples, but not all Disciples are Apostles. A Disciple is any learner who follows the teachings of another. An Apostle is one chosen and sent with a special commission from the one who sends him or her.

All followers of Jesus are Disciples because they are all learners. Jesus chose the twelve Apostles to carry on the ministry He began. All of the Apostles except Judas witnessed the resurrected Jesus. However, later Paul who may not have witnessed the resurrected Jesus, claimed to be an Apostle because he was miraculously converted on the road to Damascus where he met Jesus and received his commission (I Corinthians 15:8-9). Mary Magdalene may have also qualified to be an Apostle. She was sent by Jesus to tell the others about His resurrection. The majority of the Apostles died as martyrs. In the early church they consistently exercised a unique authority given to them by Jesus Christ. Today some people believe the office of Apostle was unique to the first century and we no longer have Apostles. Others, like Paul, believe Jesus continues to commission and send out Apostles to do His work.

A list of Disciples and Apostles can be found in Luke 6:14-16; Acts 1:13-14; the election of Matthias to replace Judas in Acts 1:26; Matthew 10:1-4; Mark 3:13-19; John 1: 35-49 mentions Nathanael; Romans 16: 7 calls Andronions and Junias Apostles; and in Acts 14:14 Barnabus and Paul are called Apostles.

Andrew

Andrew was a brother of Simon Peter and son of Jonas. He was a fisherman from Capernaum. John the Baptist directed him toward *the Lamb of God*, Jesus. He brought

Simon Peter to Jesus. Along with Philip, he was involved in feeding the 5000 with five loaves of bread and two fishes. Tradition tells us he preached in Scythia and suffered martyrdom in Achaia, being crucified on an X-shaped cross now called a St. Andrew's cross.

Simon Peter

He was the son of Jonas, and brother of Andrew. He was a fisherman and partner with James and John the sons of Zebedee. He was married (Mark 1:30 and I Corinthians 9:5) and lived in Capernaum. Peter was the most prominent and most out spoken of the Apostles and a natural leader. Jesus chose him to be in the inner circle with James and John. Peter was also present when Jesus raised Jairus' daughter from the dead, (Mark 5: 37f) was instrumental in bringing Dorcas back to life, (Acts 9:40-41) he experienced Jesus' agony in the garden, (Matt. 26:27f) and he was privileged to witness the transfiguration. (Luke 9:28f) Peter was the first to confess, *Jesus is the Christ, son of the living God*. Jesus called him *The Rock* and said upon his confession and identification with Christ, the true Rock, He would build His church. Tradition informs us he suffered martyrdom under Nero.

James

James was the son of Zebedee and Salome and elder brother of John. He was a fisherman, and one of Jesus' inner circle. He was the first martyr, being put to death by King Herod Agripa I, A.D. 44.

James, son of Alphaeus

This James was possibly Matthew's brother. Little is known about him.

John

John is the son of Zebedee and the brother of James. His mother was probably Salome (sister of Mary-mother of Jesus). He was from Galilee, and a fisherman. His family had hired servants and belonged to the employer class. John knew the high priest and was able to gain entrance to the court where Jesus was tried. He was first a Disciple of John the Baptist. John wrote the Gospel of John, the Book of Revelation, I, II, and III John. Jesus called him and James *Sons of Thunder* because of their temperament. John was in the inner circle of Jesus. According to tradition, he spent his last years in Ephesus where he cared for the mother of Jesus. John was exiled to the Isle of Patmos where he experienced the visions for the Book of Revelation. He is described as the Disciple whom Jesus loved.

Philip

Philip means *lover of horses*. He was from Bethsaida and is often characterized as being timid. He brought Nathanael to Jesus and was known for bringing Gentiles to Jesus. Philip was with the Disciples in the Upper Room before Pentecost. The best traditions say he did mission work in Asia Minor and was a great light to Asia. He was buried at Hierapolis.

Bartholomew

He was the son of Tolmai. Some think he is the same person as Nathanael. Little is known about him.

Matthew

Matthew is the son of Alphaeus, a tax collector and is also called Levi. Matthew means *gift of Yahweh*. Tax collectors were hated because they were employed by the

Roman government and often took more money than was required from the people. He invited Jesus and several tax collectors to dinner at his house. It is believed he wrote the Book of Matthew. Little else is known about him.

Thomas

Thomas was from Aram. He is also called Didymus or *the twin*. His twin is not mentioned by name. He had trouble believing in the resurrection of Jesus, so Jesus proved His identity by showing Thomas his hands and side. Thomas exclaimed *my Lord and my God*. According to tradition, he labored in Parthia, Persia and India. A place near Madras (now known as Chennai) is called St. Thomas Mount.

Simon the Zealot

Simon belonged to the Jewish patriotic party called the Zealots who were started to resist Roman aggression. They often resorted to violence. They eventually provoked the Roman war.

Judas, son of James

Some say Judas was the brother of James. Nothing else is known of him.

Judas Iscariot

This Judas is the man who betrayed Jesus. He was the treasurer for the Disciples. Jesus revealed his betrayal at the Last Supper. He identified Jesus for 30 pieces of silver, betraying Him with a kiss; but, later in remorse gave the money back and committed suicide.

Matthias

His name means *gift of Jehovah*. Matthias was chosen by lot to replace Judas Iscariot. Little is known about his ministry.

Nathanael

Nathanael means *God has given*. He was introduced to Christ by Philip. He appeared to have knowledge of the Scriptures. He and Bartholomew may be the same person.

Andronicus

He was a Jewish believer and once a prisoner with Paul.

Junias (possibly a woman)

He or she was a kinsman and fellow prisoner with Paul.

Barnabus

Barnabus was an early convert to Christianity. He sold a field and gave the proceeds to support the poor. He traveled and ministered with Paul and John Mark. Some believe he wrote the book of Hebrews.

Paul

He was an Apostle to the Gentiles. His Hebrew name was Saul. Before he was converted, he persecuted and killed Christians. He was born a Jew, a son of a Pharisee, and a member of the tribe of Benjamin. (Philippians 3.5) While on the road to Damascus, he was struck blind and asked by the Lord "Why do you persecute me?" (Acts 9:4) Saul surrendered immediately and completely to Jesus and claimed to be an Apostle. He became an aggressive missionary. He traveled extensively, making Disciples and starting churches in Galatia, Asia, Macedonia, Achaia, Rome and Spain. Tent making was his trade, and he wrote much of the New Covenant, mostly in the form of letters to the churches.

Mary Magdalene

Although she is never called an Apostle in the Bible, Mary Magdalene was sent by Jesus on a special mission, (John 20:17-18) witnessed the events of the cross and was the first to encounter the risen Lord.

Tabitha or Dorcas

She is the only woman in the Bible specifically called a Disciple. Perhaps Tabitha was a minister to widows.

Note: Much of the above information is also covered in other sections of this manuscript. The purpose for the duplication is to group the Apostles together. Therefore, in most cases references are not given here.

21st Century Perspective

The body of Christ (the church) is made up of imperfect Christians at different stages of maturity. The *church body* is compared to the *human body*. When one part is sick or hurt, the whole body hurts. Since the body is made up of parts but functions as a whole, we must love and care for even the most uncomely parts.

TO PONDER:

The Apostles and early Disciples had gifts that brought the church into being and sustained it through the ages. There are four functions which enable the church to carry out Christian ministry: Serving, Teaching, Worshipping and Witnessing. God puts together a group of people who are equipped to carry out His plan. Because we are given gifts for His purpose, we may find our gifts change over time. Read the following Scriptures and answer the questions: I Corinthians 12:8-11 and 12:28-31; Romans 12:6-13; Ephesians 4:11-14

- ❖ What are your gifts?

- ❖ How are your gifts being used?

- ❖ Have your gifts changed over the years? If so, how?

Part Two, Chapter Two, Lesson Twenty-Eight

LESSONS FOR WOMEN FROM EARLY CHURCH WRITERS

PAUL AND WOMEN

Paul came from a strict Pharisee background, (Acts 23:6) and had undoubtedly prayed the prayer, *thank God I am not a woman*, many times. Therefore, the wonder is not the content of what Paul teaches women, but that he considered women worthy of being taught at all. After Paul's dramatic conversion experience, (Acts 9:1-22) Paul came to acknowledge there was no difference between the male and female in Christianity. (Galatians 3:28) "Paul was a witness that Jesus was living. As he says: *have I not seen Jesus Christ our Lord?* He ranked himself as a personal witness to the truth on which his future career rested; and this change of mind and life came on him suddenly like a flash of lighting." (*Contemporary Thinking About Paul*, p. 125.) Paul, being acquainted with the life of Jesus, followed His example and treated women as equals.

After his conversion, Paul set about spreading the Gospel and establishing churches with the same zeal with which he had once gone about persecuting the Christians. As the churches began to grow, problems and questions arose, and Paul soon found himself in the position of helping the churches overcome their difficulties. Therefore, the letters Paul wrote are in response to questions and difficulties the churches were experiencing.

An exhaustive review of the books written by Paul and a list of the women he wrote about is included in the concordance at the beginning of this section, pages 97-122.

> **21st Century Perspective**
>
> **Paul worked side-by-side with women in the 1st century church. According to Paul, women served well. If the early church women are an indication of the way women should serve today, women would be allowed to serve in virtually every position the church has to offer.**

TO PONDER:

After reviewing the books of the Bible written by Paul, James, Peter and possibly others:, think about the following:

- ❖ What are your thoughts about women in ministry?

- ❖ How was first-century Christian women held accountable for their faith?

- ❖ How did Paul relate to women in ministry?

- ❖ How did the writer (s) of Hebrews, I Timothy and II Timothy relate to women in ministry?

- ❖ How did James relate to women in ministry?

- ❖ How did Peter relate to women in ministry?

- ❖ How did the writer of Jude relate to women in ministry?

Part Two, Chapter Three, Lesson Twenty-Nine

WOMEN IN LEADERSHIP ROLES

THE COVENANT WOMAN

TABITHA OR DORCAS

Acts 9:36-42

The Bible gives us this woman's name in Aramaic and Greek, either meaning *gazelle* or *roe*. Tabitha or Dorcas lived in the picturesque city of Joppa on the Mediterranean Sea about thirty-five miles from Jerusalem. She is the only woman in the Bible who is specifically said to have been a Disciple. (Acts 9:36) Dorcas served as a minister of external need: This "remarkable minister of service was so effective that the church at Joppa could not allow her to die." (*Beyond the Curse*, p 114; Acts 9:36-42) "Tabitha is depicted as serving in some of the capacities that were later associated with the office of deacon. . . so that even if she was not labeled or commissioned as a deaconess, Luke may still be presenting her as a prototype of a deaconess." (*Women in the Earliest Churches*, p. 155.) Some believe she was a widow and "widows who were among the most needy were the objects of Tabitha's charity." (*The Wycliff Bible Commentary*, p. 1142) Although her name is not mentioned, perhaps she was one of the chosen individuals to help care for the Hellenist widows. (Acts 6:1) She is said to have been full of good works and acts of charity.

We are not told what caused Dorcas' death. The attending women prepared her body for burial by washing it and placing it in an upper room. The disciples at Joppa sent for Peter who was about 10 miles away in Lydda. Perhaps her friends had faith that through Peter God would work a miracle and bring Dorcas back to them. No doubt, they had heard or seen the miracles being performed through Peter. (Acts 5:12-16) The widows were grieving and showing each other the garments that Dorcas made. Apparently she was an exceptional seamstress. While widows' garments would have been somewhat drab, women's dresses in that time were long, one piece, garments woven to fit the individual with a girdle of silk or wool in rainbow colors with a fringe from the waist to the ankles. The headdress was a cloth pinned over a cap set with pearls, silver, gold or other ornaments. A married woman wore coins or ornaments on the front of her cap to show her dowry. Often a tightly fitting jacket of scarlet covered with tapestry or fine needlework was worn over the tunic or long dress. Women completed their attire with earrings and other jewelry. Peter warned against too much outward adornment. (I Peter 3:3-4) It was reported Christians of the first-century also "adopted unadorned, simple styles. These styles set them apart from unbelievers and symbolized their commitment to a life of humble service to God." (*Bible Illustrator*, Winter, 1986, p. 23)

Dorcas is still honored for her needlework. "Out of this first work of hers grew the Dorcas Sewing Societies, now world-wide." (*All The Women Of The Bible*, p. 219.)

When Peter arrived, he put everyone out of the room, knelt and prayed; then turning to the body said, "*Tabitha, rise.* And she opened her eyes, and when she saw Peter she sat up. And he gave her his hand and lifted her up. Then calling the saints and widows he presented her alive." (Acts 9:40-41)

Peter was in Joppa for several more days and stayed at the house of Simon the tanner where he experienced the vision about God making the *unclean* animals *clean*. The vision was interpreted to mean the Gentiles were now acceptable to God. "And Peter opened his mouth and said: *Truly I perceive that God shows no partiality, but in every nation any one who fears him and does what is right is acceptable to him.*" (Acts 10:34-35) Tabitha or Dorcas, Jew or Greek, was acceptable. She was a beautiful person adorned on the inside and adorned on the outside with her beautiful garments. She was a gifted and talented Disciple who used her gifts and talents for the benefit of others and for the glory of God.

LYDIA

Acts 16:14-15, 40; Philippians

Paul, the radical Jew and Roman citizen who once dragged Christian women and men before the courts to be imprisoned for their faith, had become a radical Christian barreling forth with the Gospel and establishing churches: "He arrived in Philippi in late summer or early autumn of AD 48, having tramped across Western Turkey from Galatia." (*Paul, A Critical Life*, p. 211.) Paul was on his second missionary journey. Philippi was named for Phillip II of Macedon who was the father of Alexander the Great. "The city was the civic and administrative center of an area of some 2,100 sq km (730 sq. miles). The vast majority of the settlers lived on their land, but the city was the market for their produce, and the source of services and manufactured goods." (Ibid., 212) The people of the region spoke Latin and Greek. Archaeological evidence shows the people worshipped Egyptian gods and Roman deities. "Perhaps there was a small Jewish population. By law, the Jews had the right to have a place of worship. All known first-century Diaspora synagogues were within cities." (*Paul, A Critical Life*, p. 213) There was a school of medicine at Philippi and it is possible Luke attended school there. Luke took pride in reporting that Philippi was the leading city of the district. (Acts 16:12)

It was on the Sabbath when Paul and his missionary party went outside the city gate by the river to find a *place of prayer*; perhaps a synagogue. (Acts 16:11-40, Notes, RSV.) They found a group of women who had come together to worship and pray. Paul told the gathering the story of Jesus. A woman by the name of Lydia, perhaps the leader of the group, accepted Jesus as her Lord and Savior. She was a business woman from the city of Thyatira who sold purple cloth and garments. There were more trade guilds in Thyatira than any other Asian city and "we can be sure Lydia belonged to an important group, the Dyers' Guild." (*All The Women of the Bible*, p. 224.) While she may have sold the cheaper dye product called *turkey red* made from the madder-root, she could have sold garments dyed with the more expensive dye obtained from murix shells and ocean mollusk. Regardless of the origin of the dye, her business catered to the rich, and she made a very good living. The fact that she was in Philippi, some 500 miles away from her hometown suggests her trade was an important export.

Nothing is said of Lydia's marital status. She may have been single and never married or a widow or even divorced. What we are told is she was the mistress of her own household, she employed servants, and her home was large enough to accommodate the entire missionary party who stayed with her while in Philippi.

When Lydia became a Christian, her entire household followed her lead. She not only became the first Christian in Europe, but her home became the meeting place for the first church in Europe. (Acts 16:40) "We do not know how many converts there were in Philippi at that time, but we do know that they chose Lydia's house as their meeting place." (*Women of the Bible*, p.112.) "Paul, in contrast to his Jewish background, is willing to begin a local church with a group of women converts." (*Women in the Earliest Churches*, p. 148.) Later Paul wrote a letter to the

Philippians shedding light on the newly formed church. Paul's main objective was to win people to Christ. However, he soon found Christians needed instructions on how to live as Christians. In Paul's letters to many of the churches, he addressed problems. But, in the Philippian letter, (there were likely more letters to the Philippians) (*Paul, A Critical Life*, pp 215-221), did not deal with church problems. In fact, the Philippian letter is full of joy and thankfulness. The Philippian church showed an understanding of Paul's missionary work and even sent a gift to support the work. Paul said they had been *partners in the gospel from the first day*. (Philippians 1:5)

Euodia and Syntyche were having some kind of disagreement. Paul urged these two women to *agree in the Lord*. (Philippians 4:2) and said they had labored side by side with him in the gospel. Women were definitely active participants in the Philippian church and likely the founders and sustainers of the church. Paul was happy with their work. He says of them: "And you Philippians yourselves know that in the beginning of the Gospel, when I left Macedonia, no church entered into partnership with me in giving and receiving except you only; for even in Thessalonica you sent me help once and again. Not that I seek the gift; but I seek the fruit which increases to your credit. I have received full payment, and more; I am filled, having received from Epaphroditus the gifts you sent, a fragrant offering, a sacrifice acceptable and pleasing to God. And my God will supply every need of yours according to his riches in glory in Christ Jesus." (Philippians 4:15-19)

The seed that was first planted in Lydia took root and became a blessing not only to Paul, but to Philippi and to Europe.

PRISCILLA OR PRISCA

Acts 18: 1-19 and 24-28; Romans 16:3-5; I Corinthians 16:19; II Timothy 4: 19

Priscilla is always mentioned with her husband Aquila who was said to have been a Jewish Christian from Pontus, a large province of northern Asia Minor (modern Turkey) along the coast of the Black Sea. It is believed Peter may have evangelized the area. He addressed a letter to the exiles of the Dispersion in Pontus. (I Peter 1:1) Perhaps Priscilla and Aquila became believers in Jesus as Messiah while living among the exiles in Dispersion. This couple shared a unique closeness as they lived, worked, ministered and traveled together. They may have gone to Rome, at first, in order to establish their tent-making business. Travel was made easier by paved roads and freighter ships. Business people were expected to travel. The raw materials of Cilician cloth or crude leather for tents would have been easily accessible in Rome. Many Jews had traveled to Rome, so many in fact that in A.D. 49, Claudius issued an edict expelling the Jews from Rome. (Acts 18:2) Priscilla and Aquila were among the Jews forced to leave.

Priscilla and Aquila sailed some 400 to 500 miles across the Mediterranean Sea to Corinth where they met Paul who came from Athens. Priscilla and Aquila must have arrived first because they seem to have been established in their home and trade when Paul arrived. The shop where they worked was likely a "covered gallery running round all four sides of a square. It would have had a uniform height and depth of thirteen feet. The width varied from eight feet to thirteen feet. There was no running water or toilet facility. In one of the back corners, a series of steps in stone or brick followed by a wooden ladder to a loft lit by an open window centered above the shop entrance, which at night was closed by wooden shutters. Prisca and Aquila made their home in the loft, while Paul slept below amid the tool-strewn work-benches, rolls of leather and canvas. (*Paul, A Critical Life*, p.263.)

Having much in common with them, being a Jewish Christian and a tent-maker, Paul found fellowship and hospitality with Priscilla and Aquila and ended up staying with them in their home for a year and a half. During this time, Paul taught in the synagogue, and there is no reason to believe Priscilla and Aquila and the other Jewish Christians did not attend the synagogue as well. In 70 A.D. when the temple was destroyed and the synagogues were eventually closed to Christians, the home church became more established as a place of worship for Christians. The early theologian Tertullian reports: "By the holy Prisca, the gospel is preached." (*All The Women of the Bible*, p. 229.)

As Paul sailed for Syria, he took Priscilla and Aquila with him, leaving them off at Ephesus. (Acts 18:19) The Scriptures tell us they were still attending the synagogue in Ephesus. There they heard an eloquent, but uninformed, speaker by the name of Apollos: "When Priscilla and Aquila heard him, they took him and expounded to him the way of God more accurately. . . . [then] Apollos powerfully confuted the Jews in public, showing by the scriptures that the Christ was Jesus." (Acts 18:26, 28)

It is clear Aquila and Priscilla had a church in their home in Ephesus. Paul wrote to the church at Corinth from Ephesus: "Aquila and Prisca, together with the church in their house send you hearty greetings in the Lord." (I Corinthians 16:19) Apparently some ten to fifteen years later Priscilla and Aquila were again in Rome where they were continuing to spread the good news of Jesus. Paul, while in Corinth, wrote to the Roman church: "greet Prisca and Aquila, my fellow workers in Christ Jesus, who risked their necks for my life, to whom not only I but also all the churches of the Gentiles give thanks; greet also the church in their house." (Romans 16:3-5)

There is no doubt these quiet, consistent, Mediterranean missionaries were very effective in spreading the Gospel. They were not only good preachers and teachers, but they appeared to have loved and cared for their fellow Christians—even *risking their necks* for some!

PHILIP'S DAUGHTERS

(2ND Generation Evangelist)

Acts 6: 1-7; Acts 21: 8-9

Philip (lover of horses) was a Greek-speaking Jew who was full of the Holy Spirit and wisdom. (Acts 6:2) He was one of seven men chosen to minister with Greek widows and the poor. These men were credited with having been the first deacons. They not only served tables, but taught the Word of God and performed the duties of administration. (Philippians 1:1; I Timothy 3:8-13)

At first, nothing is mentioned about Philip's family. However, it is possible they went with him when the church was dispersed following the stoning of Stephen. Except for the Apostles the church in Jerusalem was scattered throughout the region of Judea and Samaria. (Acts 8:1) Philip went to Samaria where his ministry was highly successful. Many miracles were performed through him. Among his converts was Simon the magician of Samaria (Acts 8:9-13) and the Ethiopian eunuch. (Acts 8:26-40) Therefore, Philip is credited with beginning a ministry to the African continent and he would have been a forerunner of Peter and Paul in preaching to the Gentiles. After Philip baptized the eunuch, the Lord caught Philip up and the eunuch saw him no more and later Philip was found in Azotus on the Mediterranean Sea coast. (Acts 8:39-40)

Philip began his ministry in Jerusalem, preached in the villages of Samaria, was instructed by the Holy Spirit to go to a road between Jerusalem and Gaza where he met the eunuch, was whisked away to Azotus, traveled through the towns, preaching as he went until he came to Caesarea, Palestine on the coast of the Mediterranean Sea about 25 miles from Samaria where he had a house and a family. Caesarea is also the place where Peter preached to Cornelius, the Centurion, who received Christ. When the believers and the circumcised saw this "they were amazed because the gift of the Holy Spirit had been poured out even on the Gentiles." (Acts 10:45)

It was under these circumstances and in this Roman military, harbor town that Philip's daughters prophesied. The function of a prophet is to "speak the words that God puts in his mouth." (Deuteronomy 18:18) "After Pentecost, the differentiation between the sexes with regards to prophetic gifts was removed." (*Pictorial Bible Dictionary*, p. 690.) Following Pentecost, Peter preached the first Christian sermon, saying:

"but this is what was spoken by the prophet Joel: *And in the last days it shall be, God declares, that I will pour out my Spirit upon all flesh, and your sons and your daughters shall prophesy, and your young men shall see visions, and your old men shall dream dreams; and yea, and on my menservants and my maidservants in those days I will pour out my Spirit; and they shall prophesy.*" (Acts 2:17-18) The gift of the Spirit to all Christians was seen as a mark of the Messianic Age.

When Paul, the great missionary who once persecuted the Christians, came to Caesarea, he stayed with Philip and Philip's daughters. (Acts 21:8-9) "Paul took it entirely for granted that women were ministers of the church in precisely the same sense as men. He recognized their gifts as fruits of the Spirit, which he had neither the desire nor the authority to oppose." (*Paul, A Critical Life*, p. 289)

These four daughters of Philip were second-generation Christians, following in the footsteps of their father, carrying the Gospel of Jesus Christ forward. Without the proclamation of the Gospel by the next generation, the Gospel would surely be lost.

PHOEBE

Romans 16:1-2

In Romans 16, RSV, Phoebe is identified as a *deacon* from Cenchrea. Both the KJV and NIV render the passage *servant*; the Living Bible calls Phoebe *a dear Christian woman*. The word interpreted in this passage is exactly the same word used for a male deacon, *diakonos* which means she was a female minister or female deacon. "It was not until the fourth century A.D. that the word 'diakonissa' was used. (*Ministry of Women in the Early Church*, p. 138.) I Peter 4:10-11 tells of two kinds of ministry or service:

"As each has received a gift, employ it for one another, as good stewards of God's varied grace: whoever speaks, as one who utters oracles of God; whoever renders service, as one who renders it by the strength which God supplies; in order that in everything God may be glorified through Jesus Christ. To him belong glory and dominion for ever and ever, Amen."

Everyone has received a gift. Ministers who are verbally oriented are those who equip the saints: Ephesians 4:11 lists those people as being apostles, prophets, evangelists, pastors, and teachers. Those who are given to service perform good deeds and hospitality. Men and women, alike, are encouraged to participate in both kinds of ministry. When *diakonos* refers to a man it is always translated *minister*. In the Living Bible when the word is used about Timothy, he is called *a worthy pastor*. (I Timothy 4:6) The RSV renders the word *minister*. Therefore the question remains: Was Phoebe a pastor who equipped the saints or was she one who ministered through good deeds and hospitality?

It is difficult to know exactly when ministry and service became offices in the church. Women often performed the task of assisting others with material aid or money. (*Women in the Earliest Churches*, p.151) It is believed the office may have had its beginnings when the seven men were chosen to assist and care for the Greek widows. (Acts 6:1-3) It is clear many women served in this capacity. However, Phoebe is the one given the title. Paul entrusted Phoebe with a letter to be given to the church at Rome. It is unclear as to whether Phoebe was going to Rome for another reason and delivered the letter as a favor to Paul or whether she went to Rome as a special missionary in order to assist the Roman church.

Paul tells us Phoebe was a leader, if not the leader of the church in Cenchrea, about eight and one-half miles east of Corinth—"the most important harbor of Corinth's three harbors." (*Pictorial Bible Dictionary*, p. 182) "Harbor towns of that period were extremely wicked places." (*All The Women of the Bible*, p. 231.) "Paul may have founded the church on his second missionary journey." (*Pictorial Bible Dictionary*, p.150.) He stopped there and had his hair cut in fulfillment of a vow he made. (Acts 18:18) It is obvious Paul knew Phoebe well. She must have been a strong and courageous lady. He highly recommended her to the Roman church and asked the church to stand by her and assist her in whatever she needed: "The Romans are to be at Phoebe's disposal because she has been a leader over many and even over Paul! No other person is called *prostatis* in the New Testament. The verb form of *prostatis* which is *proistemi*, literally signifies *to stand, place before or over.*" (*Beyond the Curse*, pp. 115-116.)

Rome was cosmopolitan and multi-cultural. Women were slightly more advantaged there than in Athens, Greece and slightly less advantaged there than in Macedonia, Asia Minor and Egypt. (*Women in the Earliest Churches*, pp. 10-23) In Macedonia, "women were in all respects the men's counterparts. They played a large part in affairs, received envoys, and obtained concessions from them for their husbands, built temples, founded cities, engaged mercenaries, commanded armies, held fortresses, and acted on occasion as agents or even co-rulers. . ." (*Hellenestic Civilization*, p. 74.)

Phoebe was not a novice. She was given the responsibility for delivering an important letter and traveled more than 600 miles to deliver it. She may have joined a caravan and traveled mostly by land which would have been more acceptable for a woman traveler in that day. (*All The Women of the Bible*, p. 230.) On the other hand, she may have sailed from her hometown port by way of the Saronic Gulf. Perhaps Paul was able to advise her about traveling by sea. He had traveled from the port of Chenchrea on his way to Ephesus. (Acts 18:18)

The Bible tells us nothing of Phoebe's later work. Although the church at times has tried to eliminate the service of women, (*Women in the Earliest Churches*, p. 200.) the office of servant and the service itself have persevered. In the "Ante-Nicene Fathers Papers," (7, 1975, p.492), there is an ordination ceremony for the deaconess dating between A.D. 350-400:

"O Eternal God, the Father of our Lord Jesus Christ, the Creator of man and of woman, who didst replenish with the Spirit Miriam and Deborah, and Anna, and Huldah; who didst not disdain that Thy only begotten Son should be born of a woman; who also in the tabernacle of the testimony, and in the temple, didst ordain women to be keepers of Thy holy gates, --do Thou now also look down upon this Thy servant, who is to be ordained to the office of a deaconess, and grant her Thy Holy Spirit and 'cleanse her from all filthiness of flesh and spirit' that she may worthily discharge the work which is committed to her to Thy glory, and the praise of Thy Christ, with whom glory and adoration be to Thee and the Holy Spirit forever. Amen" (*Women in the Earliest Churches*, p. 200)

There is no doubt Phoebe and many others like her held important roles of service and ministry and their service was instrumental in the growth of the infant church: The question of women's ordination is not discussed in the New Covenant, but there is nothing in the material that rules out such a possibility. Perhaps less emphasis should be given to position and more emphasis given to actual service. "If the possibilities for women in the earliest churches, as evidenced in the New Testament, should be seen as models for church practice in subsequent generations then it should be seen that women in the New Testament era already performed the tasks normally associated with ordained clergy in later eras." (*Women In the Earliest Churches*, p. 220.)

MARY OF ROME

Romans 16:6

In 56 A.D. Rome was a city of "over a million people with no street signs and no house numbers." (*Paul, A Critical Life*, p. 359) It would have been a difficult city to navigate if one was not familiar with the area. Phoebe, a deacon of the church at Cenchreae, went to Mary's church with a letter from Paul. Apparently there was more than one house church in Rome. When Paul wrote to the church at Rome he also greeted Prisca and Aquila and *the church in their house.* (Romans 16:5) We know Mary was a member of the Roman church to whom the letter was addressed because she had *worked hard among them.* (Romans 16:6) It appears the church was without a designated leader at the time. Paul wrote: "I myself am satisfied about you, my brethren, that you yourselves are full of goodness, filled with all knowledge, and able to instruct one another." (Romans 15:14) Perhaps Mary was one of the members of the church able to instruct others. We are not told about her work, only that she worked hard. Nothing is said about her family, whether she was married, single or divorced or if she had children or if she was wealthy or poor. "Wealth had brought women in Rome a surprising degree of freedom, a variety of occupations was open to them, and they could be divorced and they could inherit property." (*Women of the Bible*, p. 305.) We don't know if Paul knew her personally of if he had just been told about her. Perhaps Priscilla and Aquila told Paul about Mary. They had been in Rome some fifteen years earlier. There is also a chance Paul heard of Mary from the mother of Rufus with whom Paul seemed to have had a close relationship. (Romans 16:13) Rufus' mother was possibly the wife of Simon of Cyrene, the man who carried the cross for Jesus. A man named Rufus is mentioned as having been the son of Simon of Cyrene. (Mark 15:21)

It is uncertain as to when Mary's church at Rome was established. However, it is believed the church was made up mostly of Gentile members. Mary likely worked alongside a woman who was married to Andronicus named *Tryphosa* or *Junia*. "How striking then that Paul identifies Junia, a woman, as a prominent missionary evangelist, who was *in Christ before me*." (Romans 16:7; *Women of the Bible*, p 309.) In his letter, Paul wants the Roman Church to know they have the same benefits as Jewish Christians.

"Blessed are those whose iniquities are forgiven, and whose sins are covered; blessed is the man against whom the Lord will not reckon his sin. Is this blessing pronounced only upon the circumcised, or also upon the uncircumcised? We say that faith was reckoned to Abraham as righteousness. How then was it reckoned to him? Was it before or after he had been circumcised? It was not after, but before he was circumcised. He received circumcision as a sign or seal of the righteousness which he had by faith while he was still uncircumcised. The purpose was to make him the father of all who believe without being circumcised and who thus have righteousness reckoned to them, and likewise the father of the circumcised who are not merely circumcised but also follow the example of the faith which our father Abraham had before he was circumcised. The promise to Abraham and his descendants, that they should inherit the world, did not come through the law but through the righteousness of faith." (Romans 4:7-13, RSV)

Paul had a high regard for the women and their ministries in the Roman church. He could not have known of the hardships he or the Roman Christians would face in the future when he wrote these words to the Roman church: "Let every person be subject to the governing authorities." (Romans 13:1)

The governing authorities would soon have a perilous effect on the Christians in Rome. Nero's father, Claudius who had expelled the Jews, died when Nero was three years old. This is when many of the Jewish Christians such as Priscilla and Aquila were able to go back to Rome. Nero's mother, Agrippina, was a power hungry murderous woman. She married her uncle and maneuvered her son, Nero, into position to inherit the crown. She then poisoned her husband. Nero became Emperor at age sixteen and his mother directed the affairs of the state. When Nero decided to divorce his wife, Octavia, and marry a freedwoman, Agrippina threatened to take his crown away. That is when Nero followed his mother's example and had his competition poisoned. Agrippina, wishing to regain her son's favor, became his mistress. This incestuous relationship did not last long and Nero had his mother assassinated. Nero never mentally recovered from these events. (*Collier's Encyclopedia*, Vol. 17, pp. 305-306.)

Some say the fire of A.D. 64, in Rome, was set by professional arsonists who were trying to overthrow Nero. The fire, which was started near the Imperial Palace, was at first attributed to Nero. To defend himself, Nero blamed the Christians for setting the fire. When the fire was finally stopped only four of the city's fourteen districts were standing. (*Contemporary Thinking About Paul*, p. 171.)

To punish both men and women Christians and to exonerate himself, Nero made a spectacle of the Christians in Rome. "They were not only put to death, but subjected to insults, in that they were either dressed up in the skins of wild beasts and perished by the cruel mangling of dogs or else put on crosses to be set on fire, and as day declined, to be burned, being used as light by night." (Ibid. p. 171.)

Perhaps Mary was among the Christians in Rome who experienced the fire and the persecution that followed, or perhaps she was among the Christians who perished for their faith. We are not told. However, we do know Paul was beheaded in Rome. His tomb is in the Ager Vaticanue where Nero burned the Christians as human torches. (*Contemporary Thinking About Paul*, p. 171.) Paul was apparently imprisoned in Rome twice. He wrote to Timothy, "At my first defense no one took my part; all deserted me." (II Timothy 4:16) Apparently Mary and the Roman church did not help him. Perhaps the political conditions and the hardships brought on by the fire just made it too volatile. One can only imagine if Mary and her fellow church members were still alive; they were frightened, destitute and perhaps even in hiding. Yet because of them and others like them, the Christian message lives on!

NYMPHA

Colossians 4:15

When Christians no longer attended the synagogues, the house church was the main meeting place for Christians until the middle of the second century. Each church was hosted in a home with between fifteen and thirty friends and family attending including the servants and slaves. There was little formal organization. Men and women served in positions of leadership in these small congregations. Although there may have been several small groups meetings in a particular city, Paul always referred to them as *the church at*____. Paul considered all Christians to be a part of the universal church.

Nympha had a church in her house in Laodicea or perhaps in Colossea. Paul greeted her in his letter to the Colossians. He asked that the Colossians and the Laodiceans exchange letters. Unfortunately, the letter to Laodicea is not available. (Notes, Colossians, RSV) Laodicea was a wealthy city in Asia Minor situated on one of the great trade routes. The Laodiceans were famous for their banking industry and for superior black wool. There was also a medical school there, and they manufactured a famous eye salve. In 60 A.D. a great earthquake destroyed much of the city which was rebuilt with the help of the banking industry. (*Pictorial Bible Dictionary*, p. 476) Since the letter was written in the early 60's, (Introduction, Colossians, RSV) Nympha and her church would certainly have been aware of the repercussions of the earthquake.

Whether the church at Laodicea in the 60's was anything like the church at Laodicea in the 90's is debatable. In Revelation, John gives a description of the church in the 90's. The church at Laodicea was "lukewarm, rich and seemingly self-sufficient, but they didn't know they were wretched, pitiable, poor, blind and naked. Even so, Jesus loved them, reproved and chastened them and asked them to repent." (Revelation 3:14-21)

Nympha may have been a man (KJV) or a woman (RSV). The likelihood of Nympha being a woman is very good. There appeared to be many women, especially women with money and a large house who hosted house churches. (Romans 16:5; I Corinthians 16:19; Philemon 2, Acts 16:14-15, 40) "And it was a woman's house which formed the headquarters of the Jerusalem Church." (*Evangelism In The Early Church*, p. 175.; Acts 12:12) We are not told if Nympha was the leader of the church in her house.

> ### 21st Century Perspective
>
> In the 1st century women were busy being evangelist, pastors, ministers, teachers, missionaries, hostess of churches in their homes and just plain hard workers for their Lord. Paul commends them, greets them and depends on them. The early church needed women leaders and the church needs women leaders today.

TO PONDER:

Read Romans 12:6-13 and think about the following:

- ❖ Who are the women leaders in your church?

- ❖ What positions do women leaders have in your church?

- ❖ How does the leadership ministry in your church compare with the leadership ministry of the women in the first-century?

- ❖ Where have you been called to be a leader?

Part Two, Chapter Four, Lesson Thirty

WOMEN IN SUPPORT ROLES

The Covenant Woman
MARY, MOTHER OF JOHN MARK

Acts 12:5-17

Some ten to twelve years after Jesus ascended into Heaven, about 44 A.D., Christians were being ostracized by Jews and harassed or killed by King Herod Agrippa. James, the son of Zebedee, was martyred and Peter was arrested and put in prison. (Acts 12:1-3)

It was under these extreme conditions that the mother of John Mark provided a place of prayer for the early Jerusalem church. "That Luke points out that Mary would hold such a meeting in a time of mounting opposition in Jerusalem to the Christian movement is evidence that Luke is portraying one woman's courageous contribution to the community of faith." (*Women in the Earliest Churches*, p. 147.) Because Peter had been put in prison, people gathered at Mary's home to pray for him: "Earnest prayer for him was made to God by the church." (Acts 12:5)

An *angel of the Lord* rescued Peter from prison and set him free. When Peter realized what had happened, he went to Mary's house where a maid by the name of Rhoda answered the door of the gateway. She became so excited she didn't let Peter in, but ran back to tell the others. They too had difficulty believing Peter was really standing at the door and preferred to think it was his ghost. However, Peter persisted to knock and they eventually realized their prayers had been answered. Peter told them his story of escape and asked them to inform James and the brethren. "The conversion of James (the brother of Jesus) apparently took place as a result of a special appearance of Jesus to him after the resurrection." (I Corinthians 15:7) He appears early as the head of the church in Jerusalem. (Acts 12:17; 21:18; Galatians 1:19; 2:9,12; *Pictorial Bible Dictionary*, p. 401.)

We are not told about Mary's husband or about how Mary earned her living. Perhaps she was a widow. Her son, John Mark, most likely lived with her there on the western hill of Mount Zion. It is apparent she was a woman of some means as evidenced by the size of her home and servants: "Many were gathered together and were praying." (Acts 12:12; Acts 12:13) Her faithfulness was manifest in her son, John Mark, who became a missionary and traveled with Paul and Barnabas (Acts 12:25) and later wrote the Gospel of Mark, which was the *first of the four Gospels* to be written. (Introduction, Gospel of Mark, RSV.) "Tradition declares that Mark founded the church in the Jewish-Greek city of Alexandria." (*All The Women Of The Bible*, p.212)

Mary may have been related to Barnabas, and she must have been very proud of her son as she watched him grow in the faith under his care. (Colossians 4:10) Although Mary appears to be obscure, she was instrumental in consistently maintaining the Christian faith by laying foundations for the building of the church. "The effectual fervent prayer of a righteous man [or woman] availeth much." (James 5:16, KJV)

APPHIA

Philemon; Colossians

Paul's personal letter to Philemon, Apphia, Archippus and the church that met in their home in Colossae provides insight into their lives and the letter to the Colossian church demonstrates some of the challenges that Apphia and her family faced as they sought to live the Christian life.

The King James Version refers to Apphia as *our beloved* and the Revised Standard Version addresses her as *our sister*. It is believed Apphia was married to Philemon and Archippus was their son. Archippus means *master of the house* and he was most likely the leader of the Colossian church. (Col. 4:17)

The church was established by Paul's fellow worker, Epaphras while Paul was in Ephesus during his third missionary journey. (Colossians 1:7, 12, 13; Col. 4:12) Paul did not preach in Colossae. However, through correspondence and mutual friends, Paul appears to be familiar with Apphia's family. (Col. 4:7f)

Apphia's family was of the employer class with purchased servants and a house large enough to accommodate a church. Although Colossae was famous for its purple wool, it is not known if this family was involved in the wool industry. Their slave, Onesimus, stole money from them and ran away. He encountered Paul and was converted to Christianity. Paul convinced Onesimus, *the useless*, that as a Christian, he should be useful to his master. Then Paul wrote to Apphia and Philemon that Onesimus should be forgiven and received as a brother in the Lord. Paul was not concerned with the social order of society. His concern was how to live the Christian life within the circumstances of life. Slaves or servants often found edification and equal standing in the church. After all, there was "no difference in the slave and the free" (Colossians 3:11) "Slavery continued in New Testament times, but the love of Christ seemed to militate against its continued existence." (Ephesians 6:5-9; Galatians 3:28; *Pictorial Bible Dictionary*, p.799.)

The ancient city of Colossae which was destroyed by the Turks in the twelfth century was on the south bank of the Lycus River about 50 miles from Ephesus and 11 miles from Laodicea where a church apparently met at the home of Nympha. (Colossians 4: 15, RSV, NIV) The church at Laodicea was later described by the Apostle John as being neither hot nor cold. The church in Colossae had developed false doctrines and errant ways. Apphia would certainly have been exposed to the things that were happening there since her son was the leader and the church was meeting in her home. Paul identified some things that needed to be changed. He instructed: "See to it that no one makes a prey of you by philosophy and empty deceit, according to human tradition, according to the elemental spirits of the universe, and not according to Christ." (Colossians 2:8) He also pointed out how the church was being misled:

"Therefore let no one pass judgment on you in questions of food and drink or with regard to a festival or a new moon or a Sabbath. These are only a shadow of what is to come; but the substance belongs to Christ. Let no one disqualify you, insisting on self abasement and worship of angels, taking his stand on visions, puffed up without reason by his sensuous mind, and not holding fast to the Head, from whom the whole body, nourished and knit together through its joints and ligaments, grows with a growth that is from God." (Colossians 2: 16-18)

There appears to have been a strong ascetic movement in the church. The practice of worshipping angels lasted for centuries. However, Paul tried to bring them back to the fundamentals of Christ. Whether or not Apphia was involved in the ascetic movement or the worship of angels is unknown. What we do know is that Paul considered her to be a *beloved sister in Christ*.

LOIS AND EUNICE

Acts 16: 1-5; II Timothy 1:5-3:17

This mother-daughter pair is the antithesis of the mother-daughter example found in Ezekiel 16:44-45.

THE COVENANT WOMAN

Ezekiel emphasizes just how bad Jerusalem had become and writes: "Behold, every one who uses proverbs will use this proverb about you, *like mother, like daughter*. You are the daughter of your mother, who loathed her husband and her children; and you are the sister of your sisters, who loathed their husbands and their children. Your mother was a Hittite and your father an Amorite." Perhaps Lois and Eunice would compare better to Naomi and Ruth, mother-in-law and daughter-in-law who chose the Jewish tradition over the religion of the Moabites. Lois and Eunice also demonstrated a preference for the Jewish-Christian tradition as opposed to other religions, and they took the time to teach their son, Timothy.

Perhaps both of these Jewish women were widows. One can imagine Lois took care of her grandson, Timothy, while his mother, Eunice, went outside the home to work. Nothing is said about Lois' husband, but we are told Timothy's father was a Greek. (Acts 16:1; II Timothy 1:5) A mixed marriage would not have been easy for Eunice. The Jewish religion did not look favorably on mixed marriages. (Nehemiah 13:23-25) The Greek gods were worshipped in Lystra where Lois, Eunice and Timothy made their home. It was in Lystra during Paul's first missionary journey that through Paul a man was healed who had been crippled from birth. (Acts 14:8-10) When the crowd saw the miracle, they decided Paul and Barnabas were gods and proceeded to make a sacrifice to them. Paul and Barnabas managed to stop them. Then the tides turned and Paul soon found himself stoned and dragged out of the city and left for dead. It is believed Lois, Eunice and finally Timothy became Christians during Paul's first visit to Lystra. (*Pictorial Bible Dictionary*, p. 490.; Acts 14:6-20)

On his second missionary journey while traveling with Silas, Paul took the young Timothy with them. (Acts 16:1-5)

It must have taken a great deal of faith for Lois and Eunice to allow Timothy to go with Paul. II Timothy 3:11 alludes to persecutions endured by Paul in Lystra. This mother and grandmother who had taught Timothy the Old Covenant Scriptures must have feared for their son. Paul circumcised Timothy and took him under his wing. (Acts 16:3) He often spoke of him as a son and when Timothy was lax in his duties, Paul chastised him. (II Timothy 1:8; II Timothy 2:3; II Timothy 1:6; II Timothy 4:5) Timothy was not always happy with Paul. (II Timothy 1:4; *Paul, A Critical Life*, p. 365.)

Paul relied on Timothy to check on the churches and to carry correspondence from Paul to the churches and vise versa: "Thanks to money brought by Silas and Timothy from the churches in Macedonia, Paul was soon able to devote himself entirely to preaching and missionary work. (Acts 18:5; *Paul*, p. 69.) Paul testified about Timothy: "I have no one like him, who will be genuinely anxious for your welfare. They all look after their own interest, not those of Jesus Christ. But, Timothy's worth you know, how as a son with a father he has served with me in the Gospel. [Paul's assistants] were his partners in the same work and are often mentioned by name at the beginning or the end of a letter." (*Paul*, p. 166; Philippians 2:20ff)

Lois and Eunice supported Timothy and the work he did to further the cause of the Gospel. Timothy continued in the faith where the foundation was laid by first his grandmother, Lois, and then by his mother, Eunice. (II Timothy 1:5) Perhaps the saying in this instance should read *like mother, like son*.

> **21st Century Perspective**
>
> Supporting another person takes time, patience and creativity. The gift of helping another person excel is far-reaching. Confirming, edifying, building up and supporting another person can make the difference between success and failure.

TO PONDER:

Read Romans 14:19 and I Thessalonians 5:11 and think about the following:

- ❖ Who has been your support person (s)?
- ❖ How have you been supported during your life?
- ❖ What have been the results of the support you received?
- ❖ Who are you supporting? How?
- ❖ What has been the result of your support?

Part Two, Chapter Five, Lesson Thirty-One

WOMEN'S ACTIONS THAT TEACH

SAPPHIRA

Acts 5: 1-10

Sapphira was married to Ananias. Her name is an Aramaic word meaning *beautiful*, while her husband's name is Hebrew for *Jehovah has been gracious*. The year was probably A.D. 35, a short time after the crucifixion and resurrection of Jesus Christ. Sapphira and Ananias quite possibly saw Jesus and heard him speak. The couple would have been new in the Christian faith, for everyone was new at that time. The church was still a part of Judaism and the people met together at Herod's temple in Jerusalem.

At this particular time, Peter and John were filled with the Holy Spirit, and God was doing great wonders through their ministry. A crippled man was healed at the temple gate, and Peter testified to the rulers and elders: "be it known to you all, and to all the people of Israel, that by the name of Jesus Christ of Nazareth, whom you crucified, whom God raised from the dead, by him this man is standing before you well. This is the stone which was rejected by you builders, but which has become the head of the corner. And there is salvation in no one else, for there is no other name under heaven given among men by which we must be saved." (Acts 4:10-12)

The rulers and Priest warned Peter and John to stop speaking about Jesus. Even so they continued to speak the word of God boldly. Peter and John went to their fellow Christians and told them what the chief priest and elders had said. "And when they prayed, the place in which they were gathered together was shaken; and they were all filled with the Holy Spirit and spoke the word of God with boldness." (Acts 4:31) The believers in Jerusalem were unified in mind and Spirit so those who had wealth shared with the poor.

Later, we find the Jerusalem Church in need. Paul took up a collection for them. Perhaps "it was because of their early practice of voluntary *communism* that they were left with no capital and no resources with which to meet the strain of the years ahead. Paul saw in the Gentiles readiness to help the *unity* of the one church and the rightful claim of necessitous Christians." (*Worship in the Early Church*, p. 78.)

The word *church* or *ekklesia* is first used in Acts 5:11. (*All the Women of the Bible*, p. 217.) It means *called out for public assembly*. It is used in the Old Covenant to be the *people of God* and in the New Covenant it refers to the *new people of God*. The word is used both to indicate the church at large, (Acts 5:11; 9:31; 20:28) and the local congregation of believers. (Acts 11:26, 13:1; *The Wycliffe Bible Commentary*, pp. 1132-1133.)

Along with many others, Sapphira and Ananias were inspired to sell their property. "Property rights were secured by the seller pulling off his shoe and giving it to the purchaser." (*Pictorial Bible Dictionary*, p. 227.) Barnabas, the encourager, set the example by selling a field and bringing the money to the Apostles. (Acts 4: 36-37) Perhaps Sapphira and Ananias wanted to be like the others and take part in the generous sharing, or they wanted everyone to know they were among the wealthy. But, somehow their hearts were not yet ready to give all. They wanted to look good to their fellow Christians, so they deliberately conspired to lie about how much money they received from the sale of their property. They would say their gift was the entire amount of the sale, and keep back some of the money. The sin was not that they kept some of the money. It was their money to do with as they pleased. The sin was that they lied to God and to Peter. Their self-serving attitude, wanting to look better than they were, caused their death.

First, Ananias brought their gift and laid it at the Apostles' feet, pretending to have given the full amount of the sale. He fell dead and was carried out of the temple. About 3 hours later when Sapphari came to the temple, she too dropped dead and was immediately carried out and buried. Sapphari was not held responsible for her husband's lie. She was given an opportunity to tell the truth. When she also lied, she was held to the same consequences as her husband. Equal sin deserves equal punishment regardless of gender.

The death of these two church members caused fear and awe in the congregation. It served to them and to us today as a warning against using the church as a means of self-glorification. It teaches all we are and all we have belong to God and we cannot lie our way out when we hold back from Him. Mathew 6:1-4 warns about giving in order to receive praise from our fellowman: "Beware of practicing your piety before men in order to be seen by them; for then you will have no reward from your Father who is in heaven. Thus, when you give alms, sound no trumpet before you, as the hypocrites do in the synagogues and in the streets, that they may be praised by men. Truly, I say to you they have received their reward. But when you give alms, do not let your left hand know what your right hand is doing, so that your alms may be in secret; and your Father who sees in secret will reward you."

Some lessons taught by Sapphira's bad example are:

(1) A person cannot lie to God.

(2) Giving so that others will see is not the right reason for giving.

(3) All people are held responsible for their own sins regardless of gender.

THE PHILIPPIAN SLAVE GIRL

Acts 16:16-24

"At the time of Christ, slavery was established throughout the world and interwoven even by the wisest men as a normal state of society." (*Pictorial Bible Dictionary*, p. 599.) In contrast to Lydia, the independent, wealthy business woman, Paul and Silas encountered a dependent, poor slave girl who was the very property of others. One has the feeling she was young and mysteriously beautiful. Her name is not given. Perhaps her parents sold her into slavery in order to pay a debt or her parents were slaves themselves, or she was one of the poor street children. Whatever the circumstances were that brought her to her status in life, they were not unusual: "there were thousands of slaves in the Greco-Roman world. They were the work force that fueled the economy." (*Holman Bible Handbook*, p. 745.) This slave girl was especially useful to her owners because she had a spirit of divination and "brought her owners much gain by soothsaying." (Acts 16:16) The occupation of soothsaying was highly developed by all ancient peoples. Even Hebrews practiced divination, although it was condemned by God through Moses. (Deuteronomy 18:10-12)

Paul and Silas showed no concern that the girl was a slave or that she was being used by her masters to perform the art of magic. They accepted the culture in which they lived. Paul expressed the same attitude about himself and his circumstances. He said he had learned to be content in whatever state he found himself. (Philippians 4:11) Paul and Silas might never have noticed her except she continued to follow them for many days, crying out, "these men are servants of the Most High God, who proclaim to you the way of salvation." (Acts 16:17) One would hope she understood the true meaning of *Most High God*. There is no doubt, demons recognize God. Perhaps she was converted to Christianity. However, the term *most high god* was used by pagans to refer to the highest god of their pantheon as well as Israel's God. Paul became annoyed with the slave girl, turned to her and said to the spirit of divination, "I charge you in the name of Jesus Christ to come out of her." (Acts 16:18) And, the spirit left her. We are not told about her condition after the spirit left. We only know she was no longer useful to her owners. Paul and Silas were put in prison; accused of *doing things that were unlawful*. The Roman law forbade Jews from making converts of Romans. (Acts 16:21) Although the slave girl would not have been a Roman citizen, Paul and Silas' actions interfered with the rights of her owners.

As a Christian, a slave girl would have much to gain. First, she would have gained her salvation. As a member of a Christian assembly she would have been equal with her brothers and sisters in Christ. If she did not convert to Christianity, she could have been like the man who was rid of one evil spirit only to have seven others invade his being because he did not fill the space with good. (Matthew 12:43-45)

The price of a slave was nine times the wages a laborer made in a year. Paul used the imagery of slavery to help us understand what Jesus did for us on the cross. We are purchased with a price and belong to the one who purchased us. The person who purchased us is none other than God Himself. Because we belong to God, He set us free from our sins and brought us into the family to become sons and daughters. (I Corinthians 7:21-24; Galatians 4:7) The slave girl's social status was likely not changed, but she was freed from her demon and free to become a daughter in the family of God.

Some lessons to be learned from the actions of the slave girl are:

> (1) Our social status does not excuse us or exclude us from becoming a child of God.

> (2) An encounter with God and God's people can result in a cleaner life.

CHLOE

I Corinthians 1:10-11

Paul wrote in I Corinthians 1:10-11, "I appeal to you, brethren, by the name of our Lord Jesus Christ, that all of you agree and that there be no dissentions among you, but that you be united in the same mind and the same judgment. For it has been reported to me by Chloe's people that there is quarreling among you, my brethren."

Paul visited Corinth for the first time on his second missionary journey and stayed there preaching and making Disciples for more than a year and a half. Corinth was a multi-cultural city of approximately 200,000 citizens and about a half-million slaves. There were also people of other nationalities, Jews and God-fearers in Corinth. Many of these people worshipped Poseidon, the god of the sea, because the sea had made them very wealthy. They also worshipped Aphrodite, the goddess of love. When the Jews no longer accepted Paul's message in the synagogue, "he shook out his garments and said to them, *your blood be upon your heads! I am innocent. From now on I will go to the Gentiles.*" (Acts 18:6)

It is difficult to know from which segment of the Corinthian society Chloe came. However, it is likely she was one of the wealthy heads of household. We don't know where she and her household attended church or if she attended church at all. However, we do know the Corinthian church to which Paul wrote his letter would have recognized her because he used her personal name. Apparently there were many small congregations in Corinth, each under its own leadership. They were not unified for the cause of Christ, but were competing and arguing. (I Corinthians 1:12-13)

Paul had visited Corinth twice and most likely knew many of the people there, and had written them an earlier letter that has been lost. He wrote: "I wrote to you in my letter not to associate with immoral men; not at all meaning the immoral of this world, or the greedy and robbers, or idolaters, since then you would need to go out of the world. But rather I wrote to you not to associate with any one who bears the name of brother if he is guilty of immorality or greed, or is an idolater, reviler, drunkard or robber—not even to eat with such a one." (I Corinthians 5:9-11)

Had it not been for someone in Chloe's house, Paul may never have written I Corinthians. The letter is in response to questions and concerns that *Chloe's people* addressed to Paul. We know very little about Chloe. But, we do know the people in her household were acquainted with Paul and they cared enough about the church to ask Paul for help.

Some lessons learned from Chloe's people are:

> (1) When people who are close to us make mistakes, it may be wise to bring in a more experienced person, from the outside, to deal with the problem.
>
> (2) When a person asks for help, the result may benefit people for generations to come.

DAMARIS

Acts 17:34

Paul and his missionary party went to Thessalonica and then to Beroea where *many devout Greeks and not a few of the leading women* were persuaded to believe that *Jesus is the Christ*. (Acts 17:4, 12) The angry Jews from Thessalonica went to Beroea to stir up and incite the crowds. Therefore, Paul was forced to move on to Athens, while Silas and Timothy remained in Beroea. "[Paul] argued in the synagogue [in Athens] with the Jews and the devout persons, and in the market place everyday with those who chanced to be there." (Acts 17:17) The philosophers brought him to the Areopagus [the court] which was directly above the market place. The members of the Areopagus went through a very strict screening before they were allowed to serve on the court. After they passed the screening, they were appointed for life, much like the members of the supreme court of the United States. Paul stood in the middle of the court and delivered his *Mar's Hill Sermon*. (Acts 17:22-31) There were a few people who believed Paul's message about Jesus; namely, Dionysius, the Areopagite [member of the court] and a woman named Damaris: "Damaris must have been a woman of distinction or she would not have been singled out with Dionysius. In all probability she was one of the Hetairai, constituting a highly intellectual class of woman who associated with philosophers and statesmen." (*All The Women Of The Bible*, p. 259.) The Hetairai were freed women and most likely unmarried. Wives lived more secluded lives.

Damaris was a woman who accepted Jesus Christ as her Lord and Savior. She lived in Athens, was present at the highest court in the land and was found among the

Epicurean and Stoic philosophers. Perhaps she was one of the *Greek women of high standing*. (Acts 17:12) Roman law and Greek culture had created conditions quite favorable to women, and women often held wealth in their own right and were counted among the social elite.

Athens was not a planned trip for Paul. Paul had to leave Thessalonica because of an uprising of the Jews. In his own words to the Thessalonians: "when we could bear it no longer, we were willing to be left behind in Athens alone." (I Thessalonians 3:1) On one hand, Paul may have been distracted by his concern for the Thessalonian Church. Nothing is said in the Bible about the establishment of a church in Athens. " . . . we may certainly suppose that he [Paul] failed there. . ." (*Paul*, p. 67.) On the other hand, "it seems that a Christian community was rapidly formed although for a considerable time it did not possess a numerous membership. The commoner tradition names the Areopagite as the first head and bishop of the Christian Athenians." (*New Advent, Christian Athens*, p 1.) "In the second century there must have been a considerable community of Christians in Athens, for Hygeinos, Bishop of Rome, is said to have written a letter to the community in the year 139." (Ibid., p 1-2.) Dionysios and a *holy woman* by the name of Charissa are listed among the names of martyrs from Athens.

"In 529 A.D. the schools of philosophy were closed," (*New Advent, Christian Athens*, p 2.) and thereafter Christianity had no rival in Athens. What at first, may have appeared as a failure to some was not a failure at all, but a "seed planted on good ground that brought forth a good harvest. He, who has ears, let him hear." (Matthew 13: 8-9) Damaris heard!

Some lessons learned from Damaris' actions may be:

(1) Philosophy is not a deterrent to intelligent women choosing Christ.

(2) When seeds are planted on good ground they will grow.

(3) On the human level, there may appear to have been a failure when God has planned for success beyond human sight.

21st Century Perspective

The early church opened its doors to women from every station in life. Today, the church also represents every woman. Whether we wear a business suit or jeans, a frilly dress and high hills or shorts and tennis shoes, we are all part of the sisterhood of Christ, and therefore accepted.

TO PONDER:

Read I Peter 2:11-25 and think about the following:

- ❖ What did Jesus teach us by His actions?
- ❖ What did Peter tell us about good conduct?
- ❖ Whose actions have you imitated?
- ❖ What lessons have you taught by your actions?

Part Two, Chapter Six, Lesson Thirty-Two

CONSUMMATED

CONSUMMATED

The Bible is replete with covenant language concerning marriage and how God in relationship with mankind has chosen a people to be His own. God created Eve and placed her in front of Adam, and Adam chose Eve over all other creatures to be his companion and said, "This at last is bone of my bones and flesh of my flesh; she shall be called woman, because she was taken out of man." (Genesis 2:23) Men and women are made in the image of God. From the very onset of creation a relationship was established between male and female and with God—a relationship that is not to be denied. Women are uniquely female and men are uniquely male. But when a marriage is accomplished, the image of God is more clearly seen. The family was also begun from this union: "Now Adam knew Eve his wife, and she conceived and bore Cain, saying *I have gotten a man with the help of the Lord*." (Genesis 4:1)

The marriage relationship is a prototype used to teach about mankind's relationship with God. To know God and to be known by God is intimate and intensely personal. The goal is to become one with God. Eve was separate from Adam, but she and Adam chose to become one flesh. Intimacy is much more than sex. Intimacy is the giving of oneself to and for another. Intimacy is sharing, caring and planning for the utmost good of one's companion. It is a relationship that penetrates the soul. Marriage, when sealed with intimacy, is a covenant unbroken

Our relationship with God also brings us into relationship with each other. Yes, we are born into a family; but, not the family of our choosing. We choose to be in the family of God. And, it is with that family we will live through eternity.

As Jesus was busy instructing His disciples, His mother and brothers came to speak with Him. When Jesus was told his family was there, He said, "My mother and my brothers are those who hear the word of God and do it." (Luke 8:21) In I Timothy 5:1-2 we read, "Do not rebuke an older man but exhort him as you would a father; treat younger men like brothers, older women like mothers, younger women like sisters, in all purity." The family of God is created through intimacy and so was the nation of Israel. God nurtured the faithful, Noah and his wife, Abraham and Sarah, Isaac and Rebekah, and Jacob and Leah until a people emerged who would form the Hebrew nation. God made a covenant with them where the sign of the covenant was physical male circumcision. In the New Covenant the sign of the covenant is one of spiritual circumcision for all, both male and female. (Romans 2:29) Zapporah circumcised her sons and perhaps Moses in order to keep the Old Covenant. Jesus Christ shed His blood in order to initiate the New Covenant. He said, "for this is my blood of the [New] Covenant, which is poured out for many for the forgiveness of sins." (Matthew 26:28)

Ezekiel explicitly described the intimate relationship of God with His fledging people. He wrote these words of God: "And when I passed by you, and saw you weltering in your blood, I said to you in your blood, *Live, and grow up like a plant of the field.* And you grew up and became tall and arrived at full maidenhood, your breasts were formed, and your hair had grown; yet you were naked and bare. When I passed by you again and looked upon you, behold you were at the age for love; and I spread my skirt over you, and covered your nakedness: yea, I plighted my troth to you and entered into a covenant with you, says the Lord God, and you became mine." (Ezekiel 16:6-8)

THE COVENANT WOMAN

God was a husband to Israel. (Isaiah 54:5-7) Even when Israel played the harlot and served other gods, God went after her and brought her back to Himself.

The book of Hosea is an allegory about God choosing Israel, an adulterous people, and how He courted them. Hosea reports the Lord's words: "Therefore, behold, I will allure her, and bring her into the wilderness, and speak tenderly to her. And there I will give her vineyards and make the Valley of Achor a door of hope. And there she shall answer as in the days of her youth, as at the time when she came out of the land of Egypt. And in that day, says the Lord, you will call me, *My husband*, and no longer will you call me *My Baal*, for I will remove the names of the Baals from her mouth, and they shall be mentioned by name no more. . . And I will betroth you to me forever; I will betroth you to me in righteousness and in justice, in steadfast love, and in mercy. I will betroth you to me in faithfulness; and you shall know the Lord." (Hosea 2:14-17, 19-20)

God demonstrated His love for His people by the choice of a leader for them. Moses found favor with God and knew God's glory (Exodus 33:17), confessing, "O Lord God, thou hast only begun to show thy servant thy greatness and thy mighty hand; for what god is there in heaven or on earth who can do such works and mighty acts as thine?" (Deuteronomy 3:24, RSV.) God performed mighty acts and miracles so the people would know He was God. (Jeremiah 16:21) He showed them His power over nature in the wilderness when He gave them water and food and when their clothes and shoes did not wear out. He fought for Israel (I Samuel 17:47) and gave them the Promised Land. (Joshua 3:10)

In the New Covenant Jesus too performed mighty acts and miracles. He demonstrated His power over nature by calming the sea (Matthew 8:24-27) and walking on water (Mark 6:48). He fed five thousand with only five loaves and two fish. (Matthew 14:17-20) Although rooted in the physical kingdom of David, the New Covenant kingdom that Jesus has given to His people is an eternal spiritual Kingdom. (Luke 1:31-33)

In the Old Covenant, the Song of Solomon is another graphic allegory about God's love for Israel. There is no love that can compare to the love God has for His people. In the New Covenant: "For God so loved the world that He gave His only begotten Son that whoever believes in Him should not perish but have eternal life." (John 3:16)

In the Old Covenant, Israel continued to reject God's love. (Jeremiah 9:6 and 11:9-11) Even with the fullness of time and the arrival of God's Son, the promised Messiah, on Earth, He came first to the lost sheep of Israel. (Matthew 10:5-6) While many Jews believed the Old Covenant prophecies and recognized Jesus as the Messiah, there were others who were still serving other gods. Money, power, status and tradition stood in the way and many people were blinded to the truth. Jesus said, "for the sake of your tradition, you have made void the word of God. You hypocrites! Well did Isaiah prophesy of you when he said:

This people honors me with their lips, but their heart is far from me; in vain do they worship me, teaching as doctrines the precepts of men." (Matthew 15:6-9; Isaiah 29:13-14)

The covenant one makes with God through Jesus Christ the Messiah is one of love and submission. This is compared to the marriage covenant. The man is to love his wife like Christ loved the church when He gave Himself for her. The wife is to be submissive to her husband as the church submits to Christ: "Be subject to one another out of reverence for Christ. Wives, be subject to your husbands, as to the Lord. For the husband is the head of the wife as Christ is the head of the church, his body, and is himself its Savior. As the church is subject to Christ, so let wives also be subject in everything to their husbands. Husbands, love your wives, as Christ loved the church and gave himself up for her, that he might sanctify her, having cleansed her by the washing of water with the word, that he might present the church to himself in splendor, without spot or wrinkle or any such thing, that she might be holy and without blemish. Even so husbands should love their wives as their own bodies. He who loves his wife loves himself. For no man ever hates his own flesh, but nourishes and cherishes it, as Christ does the church, because we are members of his body. For this reason a man shall leave his father and mother and be joined to his wife, and the two shall become one flesh. This mystery is a profound one and I am saying that it refers to Christ and the church; however, let each one of you love his wife as himself, and let the wife see that she respects her husband." (Ephesians 5:21-33)

This concept of love and submission goes far beyond the human concept of reciprocal partnership. It is about God's love and mankind's response to God's love.

We are to keep ourselves pure, faithful and watchful as did the five wise virgins who were waiting for the bridegroom. (Matthew 25:1-10) When Jesus returns for the church "there will be two in bed, one will be taken and the other left; two women will be grinding at the mill, one will be taken and the other left." (Luke 17:34-36)

John writes in Revelation these words: "From the throne came a voice crying, *Praise our God, all you his servants, you who fear him, small and great.* Then I heard what seemed to be the voice of a great multitude, like the sound of many waters and like the sound of mighty thunder peals, crying, *Hallelujah! For the Lord our God the Almighty reigns. Let us rejoice and exult and give him the glory, for the marriage of the Lamb has come and his Bride has made herself ready; it was granted her to be clothed with fine linen, bright and pure—for the fine linen is the righteous deeds of the saints. And the Angel said to me, write this: blessed are those who are invited to the marriage supper of the Lamb.*" (Revelation 19:5-9)

Not everyone who is invited to the marriage supper of the Lamb will go. Jesus said, "the kingdom of heaven may be compared to a king who gave a marriage feast for his son." (Matthew 22:2) Many people who were invited chose not to attend the wedding. "They made light of it and went off, one to his farm, another to his business, while the rest seized his servants, treated them shamefully and killed them." (Matthew 22:5-6) Everyone is invited regardless of status in life, but not all will be found at the wedding feast.

"For your maker is your husband, the Lord of hosts is His name; . . .." (Isaiah 54:5) Our maker is our husband and God is His name. The church is the bride. The bride is composed of both males and females. Israel is personified as female many times; but she is also personified as male. (Jeremiah 2:15) "The Spirit and the Bride say, *Come.* And let him who hears say, *Come.* And let him who is thirsty come, let him who desires take the water of life without price." (Revelation 22:17) Individuals who choose to go to the marriage supper will live in perfect union with God for all eternity. "What therefore God hath joined together, let not man put asunder." (Mark 10:9)

> ### 21st Century Perspective
>
> Our covenant relationship with God is a two-sided agreement. God gave Himself on the cross for our sins. Therefore, we are to be submissive to Him as our Husband. Anything we put before God is an idol and God made it clear—going after idols is adultery. We owe God our complete and undefiled devotion.

TO PONDER:

"Blessed is he who reads aloud the words of the prophecy, and blessed are those who hear, and who keep what is written therein; for the time is near." (Revelation 1:30)

Read the Revelation of Jesus Christ aloud, one chapter a day for twenty-two days and think about the following:

- ❖ What blessings have you received from reading this book of the Bible?

- ❖ What does it mean for you to be married to God?

BIBLIOGRAPHY

Allen, John L. Jr., *The National Catholic Reporter*, "Depart, Seducer, Full of Lies and Cunning. . ." http://www.beliefnet.com/story/42/story_4277.html

Banks, Edgar, J., et al, Contributors, *The Book of Life, System Bible Study*, John Rubin and Company, Inc., Chicago, Illinois, 1971.

Bible Teacher Kit, Abingdon Press, 1994, 201 Eighth Ave. S., Nashville, TN 37202.

Bornkamm, Gunther, Translated by D.M.G. Stalker, *Paul*, Harper and Row Publishers, New York, Hagerstown, San Francisco, London , 1971.

Brancroft-Henchey, Timothy, *Pravda.Ru*, News and Analysis On Line Publication, "Stoning to Death in the 21st Century http://english.pravda.ru/society;2002;03;20;27090.html

Bratcher, "Demons in the Old Testament", The Christian Resource Institute http://www.crescourcei.org;demon sot.html

Browning, W.R.F., *Oxford Dictionary of the Bible*, Oxford University Press, Oxford New York, 1996.

Burton, Garlinda M., Ed. et. al., *Interpreter*, Henegar, Martha, "Death and Grief", United Methodist Communications, Inc., Vol. 46, No 7, Sept. 2002.

Cayne, Bernard S., ed. Et. al, *The New Lexicon Webster's Dictionary of the English Language*, Encyclopedic Edition, Lexicon Publications, Inc. New York, 1988.

Connick, C. Milo, *Jesus, The Man, The Mission, And The Message*, Prentice-Hall, Inc. Englewood Cliffs, New Jersey, 1974.

Davies, J.G., *The Early Christian Church*, Baker Book House, Grand Rapids, Michigan, 1965.

Deen, Edith, *All The Women Of The Bible*, Castle Books, N.Y., 1955.

Docery, Davis S. ed. et. al., *Holman Bible Handbook*, Holman Bible Publishers, Nashville, TN, 1992.

Farley, Gary, *The doctrine of God*, Convention Press, 1977.

Frank, Harry Thomas, ed., *Hammond's Atlas of the Bible Lands*, Hammond Incorporated, Maplewood, New Jersey, 1977.

Green, Michael, *Evangelism In The Early Church*, William B. Eerdmann Publishing Co., 1970.

Hallo, William W. et. al. ed., *The Bible In The Light of Cuneiform Literature Scripture in Context III, Ancient Near Eastern Text and Studies*, Vol. 8, The Eawin Mellen Press, Lewiston/Queenston/Lampeter, 1990.

Halsey, William, ed. et. al., *Collier's Encyclopedia*, The Crowell-Collier Publishing Co., Great Britain, 1962.

Hendricks, William L., *The Doctrine of Man*, Convention Press, 1977.

Jewish Encyclopedia, The Kopelman Foundation, Hirsch, Emil G. Ryssel Victor, "Judges, Period of", 2002, www.jewishencyclopedia.com/view.jwp?artid=690&letter=J&Search=Deborah

Josef, Andreas, Jungmann, *The Mass of the Roman Rite*, Benziger Brothers, 1951.

Josephus, *The Jewish Antiquities*, Vol. I-XX, Josephus, A.D. 94.

Judaism 101, "The Role of Women—Women In The Synagogue", Judaism's Egalitarian World, Education, http://www.jeworld.org/segregation.htm.

Kaufmann, Kohler and Gothard, Deutsch, *Jewish Encyclopedia*, Public Domain.

Kepler, Thomas S., *Contemporary Thinking About Paul*, Abingdon-Cokesbury Press, Nashville, TN 1950.

Kubler-Ross, Elizabeth, *Living With Death and Dying*, MacMillian Publishing Co., Inc. 1981.

Kubler-Ross, Elizabeth, *Questions and Answers On Death and Dying* MacMillian Publishing Co. Inc. 1974.

Kubler-Ross, Elizabeth, *To Live Until We Say Good-Bye*, Prentice-Hall, Inc., Englewood Cliffs, NJ, 1978.

Madeleine, S. and Miller, J., *Harper's Encyclopedia of Bible Life*, Castle Books, Edison NJ, 1996.

Martin, Ralph P., *Worship In The Early Church*, William B. Eerdman Publishing Co., 1964.

"Mary Did You Know?" Michael Crawford, Published by Rufus Music Co. P.O. Box 737, Alexandria, IN, 46001 or Word Music LLC, Warner Chappell Music Inc., 10585 Santa Monica Blvd., Los Angeles, CA., 90025.

McLemore, James, D. ed. et. al., *Biblical Illustrator*, Roark, Mack C. "Introduction: I John", The Sunday School Board of The Southern Baptist Convention, Winter, 1997-98.

Metzger, B. and Coogan, M. ed., *The Oxford Guide to People and Places of the Bible*, Oxford University Press, 2001.

Moody, Raymond A., *Life After Life*, HarperCollins Publishers, Inc. 10 East 53rd Street, New York, NY 10022, 1976.

Murphy-O'Connor, Jerome, *Paul A Critical Life*, Oxford University Press, 1996.

"Near Death Experiences," wwwneardeathexperiences. com.

Orr, James, ed. et al, *The International Standard Bible Encyclopedia*, Henderickson Publishers, 1994.

Our Sunday Visitor, OSV: National Catholic Weekly Newspaper, Danielski, Deborah, "Troublesome demons still on the Church's hit list?", 2/28/1999. http://www.osv.com/periodicals/showarticle.asp?pid=263

Pfeiffer, Charles and Harrison, Everett, *The Wycliffe Bible Commentary*, The Southwestern Company, Nashville, TN 1962.

Recto, Page and Linda, N.D., PhD., *Healthy Healing and Alternative Healing Reference*, Healthy Healing Publication, 1994.

Richards, Sue and Lawrence, *Women of the Bible, The Life and Times of Every Woman in the Bible*, Thomas Nelson, Inc. Publishers, Nashville,TN, 2003.

Ross, Lillian, *Daughter's of Eve, Strong Women of the Bible*, Barefoot Books, 2000.

Safrai, Shmuel, Jerusalem Perspective Article: "The Place of Women In First-Century Synagogues", www.jerusalem perspective.com/Articles/displayarticle.asp?ID=1464.

Satlow, Michael, *Jewish Marriage in Antiquity*, Princeton University Press, 2001.

Savage, Paula A. "The Biblical illustrator", 'Greek Women's Dress', Winter, 1986, pp. 17-23.

Smith, Eddie C., Latham, Bill, *Discovering Your Spiritual Gifts, Revised*, Convention Press, 1989.

Sophia, Jessee Christi, *New Testament Apocrypha*, Vol. 1, p. 246.

Spencer, Aida Besancon, *Beyond The Curse, Women Called To Ministry*, Thomas Nelson Publishers, 1985.

Steward, James S., *The Life and Teachings of Jesus Christ*, Abingdon Press, Nashville, TN.

Strong, James, *Abingdon's Strong's Exhaustive Concordance of the Bible*, Abingdon, USA, 1980.

Swidler, Leonard, *Biblical Affirmations of Women*, The Westminster Press, Philadephia, 1979.

Switzer, David K., *The Dynamics of Grief*, Abingdon Press, Nashville TN, 1970.

Tamez, Elsa, *Jesus and Courageous Women*, Study Guide by Sallie M. Caffee, General Board of Global Ministeries, The United Methodist Church, 2001.

Tarn, w.w. and Griffith, G.T. *Hellenestic Civilization*, 1952. p. 74.

Tenney, Merrill, ed. *The Pictorial Bible Dictionary*, The Southwestern Co.,Nashville, TN   1975.

The Apocrypha, "Gospel of Nichodemus", Part 1, ch. 4.

The Catholic Encyclopedia, Vol. II, Robert Appleton Company, 1907, (update, 2003)

The Holy Bible, King James Version, Regency Publishing House, Thomas Nelson, Inc. Nashville, TN, 1973.

The Holy Bible, The New Oxford Annotated Bible With The Apocrypha, Revised Standard Version, May, Herbert, G. and Metzger, Bruce M., ed., Oxford University Press, New York, 1977.

The Living Bible, Paraphrased, Tyndale House Publishers, Wheaton, Ill. 1971.

The United Methodist Hymnal, (Book of United Methodist Worship), The United Methodist Publishing House, Nashville, TN, 1989.

Throckmorton, Burton, Jr., *Gospel Parallels, A Synopsis of the First Three Gospels*, Thomas Nelson, Inc., Nashville, TN 1979.

Unger, *Archeology and the Old Testament*, Zondervan, Publishing, 1974.

Weidman, Judith L. ed., *Women Ministers*, Harper and Row Publishers, San Francisco, 1973.

Whitehead, Brady, *Genesis To Revelation*, "Ezra, Nehemiah, and Esther," Book 7, Revised Edition, Abingdon Press, Nashville, TN, 1997.

"Wind Beneath My Wings," Warner-Tamerlane Publishing Corp., Warner/Chappell Music, Inc., 10585 Santa Monica Boulevard, Los Angeles, CA 90025-4950.

Witherington III, Ben, *Women in the Earliest Churches*, Cambridge University Press, 1988.

www.ingramcontent.com/pod-product-compliance
Lightning Source LLC
Chambersburg PA
CBHW030320080526
44584CB00012B/637